TRUST ON TRIAL:

WHOM DO YOU TRUST AND WHY?

TRUST ON TRIAL:

WHOM DO YOU TRUST AND WHY?

. . . .

Cecile T. Massé, Ph.D.

iUniverse, Inc.

New York   Bloomington

iUniverse books may be ordered through booksellers or by contacting:

iUniverse
1663 Liberty Drive
Bloomington, IN 47403
www.iuniverse.com
1-800-Authors (1-800-288-4677)

ISBN: 978-1-4401-9167-1 (sc)
ISBN: 978-1-4401-9169-5 (hc)
ISBN: 978-1-4401-9168-8 (ebook)

Printed in the United States of America

iUniverse rev. date: 12/31/2009

Dedicated to Rosaline and Eli Massé, Sr.

••

*My awe-inspiring parents who taught me how to live,
love, learn*

and trust

CONTENTS

INTRODUCTION

Why a book on trust? Here let us clarify that we are speaking of interpersonal trust as opposed to a trust in a financial sense (can the two interpretations of the same word in our language have significance?)

Before we begin our discussion on this topic, I would invite readers to count the number of times trust is referred to in all of the commercials we watch on TV. It is employed as a reason to purchase everything from toothpaste to cars. I would advocate that the advertising industry, whose main goal is to get consumers to buy things they may (or may not) need, is fully aware that the one thing missing for consumers in today's society and which they are earnestly seeking is the ability to know whom or what to trust. There obviously is a reason for this, and after reading to the end of the book, I believe that readers will be able to discern for themselves why this is so.

History. I was drawn to this topic of trust while pursuing my Ph.D. in Organizational Behavior. What was the allure of this particular topic? Perhaps I was at a point in my life when I was questioning my own ability to trust or perhaps it was more about why I had chosen to trust in my past decisions. In any case, I did pursue my interest and as my dissertation topic, I chose to monitor the trust level between the Crow Indians and the Federal Government, specifically the Bureau of Reclamation, as they negotiated for water rights on the Crow Reservation in Montana. My dissertation (or Project Demonstrating Excellence as it was known by my academic institution) was entitled "As Long as the Waters Flow: Trust on Trial." This title reflects the Crow Indians' understanding of trust, which is when an agreement is made, it is entered into as long as the waters flow and the grass is green. I do use the word "Indians" because in the process of working on my studies, many of the Indians I had spoken with related to me that it was acceptable to them to be known as Indians, as opposed to Native Americans. The Crow's word for trust (phonetically pronounced to the best of my ability) is "dee-why-him-ma-call-a-chick" which translates as "I believe in your word." Of course, the past history of the interactions between the Federal Government and Indians in general indicates that a most significant number of treaties and promises entered into by the Federal Government and the Indians were broken by the Government. Some of these "broken treaties" have occurred as late as the 1970s according to the Crow Indians (some say even more recently.) I was fortunate enough to enter into the negotiations at the very beginning of the process and monitored them over the course of one year before terminating my involvement to complete the dissertation, though the negotiations themselves continued long after that. My involvement included not only observing these negotiations but also interviewing the members of both the Crow Indian and Federal Government negotiating teams with questions and discussions addressing their own perceptions of trust. This study of trust has dominated my interest and passion to this day.

During my year's study, I visited the Crow reservation often and was received with a gentle graciousness and welcoming hospitality. Because of this gracious hospitality, I was able to immerse myself in their culture, attending church services, social functions and tribal dances. While on the Crow Agency reservation, I was the guest of a tribal woman legislator who represented the Crow Indians in Montana's State Congress. She was kind, knowledgeable, and supportive as I engaged in my research. In interacting with the Crow Indians, I found them to be congenial, considerate, and courteous. Conversely, as I traveled with the Federal Government's team and visited them in their government offices, I also found them to be accommodating, hospitable, and helpful. My time spent with both negotiating team members contributed to a better understanding of the two cultures and a clearer understanding of their past experiences with each other.

Further Studies. During and after obtaining my Doctoral degree in Organizational Behavior, I engaged in research and petitioned respondents from all walks of life, all races, both genders, all age groups, and many different nationalities to answer the questionnaires that I had administered to the negotiating team members. After tabulating and analyzing these results, I recorded a series of 4 audio cassette tapes under the general title of "Understanding Trust." These four cassettes were titled: "The Trust Factors," "A Personal Look at Trust," "Understanding Trust in Families," and "Examining Trust in Organizations." Based on the titles of the chapters in this book, it is easy to see that these recorded cassettes formed the basis for this book.

Purpose. My interest in the trust topic grew and I reached a decision to write a book. The purpose of this book is twofold: First, to examine the awareness of trust in our society by looking at several "factors" which determine how trust is experienced in our daily lives, (as explained, these factors were taken from the results of the questionnaires given to the respondents from all walks of life), and second, to encourage readers to determine for themselves three important points that need to be emphasized in understanding trust. These are 1) to be able to describe for themselves their own understanding of trust; 2) to determine what role trust has played and does play in their lives; and 3) to identify characteristics that have to be present in their lives in order for them to trust someone. Opportunities are provided in each individual chapter in this book for readers to reflect on their own experiences in the different aspects of trust being discussed. The reasoning for this format is that reflection immediately upon reading certain material can serve to generate feelings and understandings that may otherwise have unconsciously and subconsciously lain dormant within the psyche. A website has been established to provide an opportunity for readers to share some of their reflections and any insights that they may have gained through this process.

For those readers who are willing to assist in my further research into the topic of trust, please go to the www.trustontrial.com website to share your perspectives, thoughts, reflections, insights and experiences relative to the information provided in this book. The site will direct you to the appropriate page for your comments.

Intent of Book. This book is not intended to be a scholarly work or an academic exercise. It is not my intention to describe previous studies of trust or to present a new scholarly perspective on these studies. Nor is it my intent to tell anyone who or what they should trust but rather how to make the best "trust" decisions for themselves. I remain firmly convinced that neither I, nor any guru, teacher, leader, minister, counselor or whoever - has anyone else's answers. As influencers in others' lives, people in these professions can serve as role models, facilitators, supporters, and guides, but ultimately it is up to the individual to discover his/her own best answers. The lesson in the parable of the "fishing" story applies in the trusting process as it does in life – "give a man a fish and he is fed for a day, teach a man to fish and he is fed for life." Offering knowledge on the trusting process and on how best to acquire the skills needed to make sound decisions about trust is akin to teaching a person to fish. This book is written to assist readers in understanding their own concept of trust and in making better decisions about trust and other issues that matter to them. In my management and leadership classes, I have often referred to the euphemistic "Chinese curse" which states, "May you live in interesting times." Though the origin of this phrase has not been proven to be Chinese, I do believe that we are indeed living in interesting times. One only needs to look at the tremendous amount of changes occurring in our daily lives, specifically as a result of the recent economic crisis we are experiencing here in the United States, as in the rest of the world. In order to deal with these changes effectively, especially where trust is concerned, it becomes crucial to improve our own decision-making skills through engaging in effective critical thinking skills. Also necessary is to learn all we can through other sources such as listening to others who offer sound, unbiased perspectives (this suggestion is very important), discussions with knowledgeable and informed people, reading, or any other effective means of gathering information. The knowledge needed to make effective trust decisions in these times of great change combined with the development of critical thinking skills, will go a long way in making meaningful and competent trust decisions which have a tremendous impact on our lives.

Processes/Approaches. As mentioned, personal reflections on the role trust has played in our individual lives is worth the effort in laying the groundwork for making more quality trust decisions in the future. The three processes to keep in mind when considering making better trust decisions in the future are: 1) the consideration of using the Triple A Approach – being aware, being alert and taking action; 2) the need for effective critical thinking skills; and 3) the determination to effectively employ emotional intelligence as described in the book titled "Emotional Intelligence" by Daniel Goleman. These processes/approaches are discussed in more depth in the last chapter. The reader is invited to consider these approaches in reading the following chapters so that they can best relate to the discussion in the final chapter.

Instinct and Intuition. If one had to make a decision immediately as to whom or what to trust, what elements would affect the reader in making that decision? Yes, instinct and intuition do play a major role and are crucial in the trusting process. What is the difference between 'instinct' and 'intuition?' We could describe 'instinct' as a natural inclination or innate pattern of behavior. We talk about an animal's instinct to engage in certain survival, reproductive and social behavior patterns; we say they are born with these patterns. This impulse is more natural than it is a reasoning process. The same can be said of human beings – we are born with these same instinctual patterns that are inherent and innate. They can be considered as automatic responses. Like instinct, intuition is a natural tendency and/or an unconscious knowing. It usually comes in the form of a keen and quick insight. However it is important to note that intuition involves subconscious intellectual thinking…our reasoning process is involved at some level. The conclusion can be made that the more we use our intuition, the more we can refine the quality of this intuition. Consequently, the more that we pay attention to our intuition and come to trust it and rely on it, the more we can refine the quality of our intuitive insights.

If trust has been damaged or violated by an individual, an organization, or an institution, what course of action can be taken to regain a healthy perspective and sense of oneself in order to be able to trust again? It is my perception that many of us haven't really given this concept of trust much thought and therefore are not fully aware when we have made a decision to trust. We may have even less awareness as to the best course of action to take when our trust has been destroyed. Awareness will be a key factor throughout our discussions because without it, a good understanding of trust cannot be had. The goal then of this book is to explore these conditions of trust so that readers may take a firm resolve to understand how they would define trust in their lives, how they can maintain this trust once it has been achieved and what actions they would take when it is violated…in other words, to become more aware of the trust process.

The book is divided into five parts: 1) the trust premises that shape our underlying perception of trust, 2) the trust factors themselves, 3) a personal look at trust, 4) understanding trust in families, 5) examining trust in organizations and 6) what processes can be employed to enhance and improve our trust relationships.

I WANT TO THANK ALL OF MY STUDENTS…

I have taught classes in various colleges and universities both on campus and online for over 20 years and it has been a very challenging and rewarding endeavor. I have discovered in my lifetime that a good education is worth more than all the riches this world can produce, as it can bring knowledge, skills, self-confidence, and positive self-esteem. There is nothing more satisfying than to hear from students about something they have just learned in class that has made a difference in their lives for the better. There is also nothing more thrilling than watching students who have struggled with work, family and school, march down the aisle on graduation day to achieve the goal they dedicated themselves to pursuing ….a degree in the area of their choosing!

At this point, I would like to thank all of my students in the management, business and human resource courses that I have taught in various universities and colleges throughout the years. Their contributions to the information and understanding of trust found in this book have been prodigious and much appreciated. The line in the song "Getting to Know You" from the musical "The King and I" proclaims that "if you become a teacher, by your students you'll be taught", and this statement has proven to be so very accurate in my own life. Being able to teach has been the greatest blessing of my life and I've learned so much from my students. I am truly grateful to have had the opportunity to interact with them over the years, thereby enriching and blessing my life. So, to my present and all of my former students, I extend the most heartfelt and the most meaningful of "thank yous!!"

Please remember that you are invited to share your perspectives and comments on all of the questions and reflections in this book on the website: **www.trustontrial.com.**

So without further adieu, let us begin our journey of exploring this concept of trust!

CHAPTER ONE

THE TRUST PREMISES

In preparation for an excursion into such a life altering topic as trust, it is important to address the framework within which we "see" trust. What experiences shape our reactions to trust issues? With what "eyes" do we observe the human interactions that ultimately lead to trust or distrust? The eye of the beholder is molded by the experiences of the beholder and these experiences play a major role in the daily decisions to trust or distrust. Also the belief systems within which we operate, either consciously or unconsciously, contribute significantly to our interpretation of a trust situation. There appear to be overarching principles that facilitate and set the scene for the greater understanding and interpretation of this microscopic look at trust.

The intent of this chapter is to address these overarching principles, or premises, that affect our inspection and understanding of the eight factors which we will be discussing in the following chapter. The official definition of a premise is: to set forth beforehand, as by way of introduction or explanation. Some of these premises may seem self-evident and elementary, but it is surprising how many times they are ignored in favor of choosing to trust blindly. Before reflecting on the material in the following chapters, it's important to see what was "set forth beforehand" as we shaped our present assumptions on trust. These are personal understandings that exist within when examining the nature of trust.

PREMISE #1

Before you can learn to trust, you have to know who you are. "Know Thyself"

-Plato
Greek philosopher and mathematician (428–348BC)

"Know Thyself" was the motto carved in stone on the entrance of the school founded by the Greek philosopher Plato. We have all heard this saying at one point or another in our lives, perhaps with great thought, perhaps with some reflection, or perhaps with boredom. But in discussing trust, this short sentence is crucial. It is all encompassing in the sense that it sets the tone for how we see ourselves, and how we see ourselves is critical in shaping our ability to trust both ourselves and others. In the advanced civilizations of ancient history, self-understanding was highly valued and considered as the true mark of wisdom. Over the years the emphasis on self-understanding was lost in favor of the materialism that surrounds us in our daily world of living. In today's society, what others think and say is often more valued than self-knowledge and understanding. We are influenced by the media and are tempted to succumb to their manipulations to decide for us who we should be, what we should think, what we should buy, and what we should have. As we reflect on the commercials, the movies and TV shows we find that they define the values that dominate the American scene. They do this because so many people give them control over their thinking; it seems easier to accept what others say than to critically think things through for ourselves. As mentioned, we will discuss critical thinking skills further in the last chapter. In engaging in our own critical thinking process, we are able to evaluate for ourselves what is important to us and what values we subscribe to. Knowing oneself is a powerful tool in learning to accept ourselves, which supports our ability to trust effectively.

Often cited in response to the question, "What is your a favorite quote?" is this one by Shakespeare: "To thine own-self be true; and it must follow, as the night the day, thou canst not then be false to any man."-- Hamlet. Act I. Sc. 3.   But the question remains -

how can we be true to ourselves if we haven't tried to understand who we really are? In this regard, a wonderful quote from Dr. Seuss advises us to "Be who you are and say what you feel, because those who mind don't matter and those who matter don't mind." How many readers have taken on the time-consuming process of self-knowledge and self-understanding? I suspect that the answer is less than 50%. Trusting effectively is built on knowing one's self.

What was meaningful for me in learning about the Crow Indian customs, (and this is true of most American Indians) is the belief that a child comes into the world with his/her own unique strengths and talents, and once born, that child is observed by adult Indians who wait for these strengths and talents to manifest. Once they are discovered, it is the role of family and friends to do everything possible to encourage and assist in developing these strengths and talents, thereby allowing the child to "know itself." This is considerably different from today's society where parents push children toward an occupation that the parents favor – doctor, lawyer, or other well-paying professions. I'm reminded of the movie "The Natural." In the opening scene Roy Hobbes, the protagonist who is gifted in the sport of baseball, as a boy is playing "catch" with his father in the yard. His father reminds him "It's not enough to have a talent son, you must develop it." We all do come into the world with our own unique strengths and talents but sadly enough you will hear people say, even as adults, "I really don't know what my strengths or talents are." Knowing our gifts is one part of the equation, developing these gifts and talents is also essential. Knowing who we are and what our talents and strengths are is the solid foundation on which to build goals and dreams.

> "Each person's only hope for improving his lot rests on recognizing the true nature of his or her basic personality, surrendering to it, and becoming who he or she really is."
> *-Sheldon Kopp*
> *Psychotherapist (1929-1999)*

Knowing yourself is a very important action to take in choosing to trust others.

Cecile T. Massé, Ph.D.

You may wish to post your reflections or comments on www. trustontrial.com

Question: Who are you?

Reflection 1:

In answering this question, did you define yourself as part of a family, nationality, church member, or by your standing in society? Did you respond by citing your interests, likes, dislikes? Did you relate your information in terms of how secure you feel or have felt in your life?

Reflection 2:

How do you feel about the way you responded to this question? Does your understanding of who you are come mostly from others' reactions to you or from knowledge that you've discovered about yourself?

Question: What is your greatest strength? Are you using it to full advantage in your life?

Reflection: Are you able to state what you feel your strength(s) is or are? Have you developed your talents and gifts? Why or why not? How have you utilized your talents and gifts? Do you intend to develop any strengths in the near future?

PREMISE #2

Trusting others is about trusting yourself!

"As soon as you trust yourself, you will know how to live."
-Johann von Goethe
German author (1749-1832)

In following this premise, it's important to realize that every time we choose to trust, we run a risk that our trust will be violated. When we choose to trust others, we do so with the expectation that our trust will be honored and well placed. We do not trust with the idea that negative surprises will result. Consequently, we need to also trust ourselves to deal effectively with the fallout that can occur when our trust is violated. Say that I choose to trust someone with a prized possession with the expectation that no harm will come to this prized possession. In this scenario, it turns out that the person to whom I entrusted this possession actually does, (intentionally or not) harm it in some way. This premise implies that I trust myself to handle this situation without losing control of myself or the situation. Yes, I probably will feel some anger, hurt and resentment -- maybe even devastation -- when that trust is violated. My emotions will be particularly strong if the trust was violated intentionally and willfully. But I trust myself not to retaliate in any way that will harm the violator physically, emotionally or ethically. Too often in today's world, we hear of incidents in the news where a person's trust was violated and the situation ended in harm or even death to the violator. This premise states that you will feel the emotions that come from having your trust violated, but that you will not lose control of your emotions to the degree that you harm that person or yourself. We will discuss this more in the last chapter in the discussion on Emotional Intelligence. It's important to realize that a person can get through the hurt and violation of a betrayal and come out on the other side as a stronger person.

Trusting yourself can also mean that you don't just "give" your trust to someone or some situation but that you also do your own research and gain your own understanding of the issue or person at hand. If you have a financial advisor who manages investments you have made, you don't just agree with all the recommendations that s/he makes, but you do research on both the topic and the person, so that you can feel self-confident in placing your trust in this financial advisor. The same is true of your doctor, lawyer, realtor, car repairman, contractor or whatever professional you choose to deal with. However, there are times when we must trust whomever we're dealing with – for instance, when we travel. We can choose to trust an airline pilot – or not fly, we can choose to trust a taxi driver – or drive ourselves, we can choose to trust a bus driver – or find some other way to get where we're going. When we trust a professional of any kind we recognize that this person has the knowledge and expertise in their given field. However, you also recognize that you have some responsibility when you choose to put your trust in that person. Some people feel that employing the services of a doctor, psychiatrist, counselor or other professional that can have a strong influence in their lives is the "luck of the draw." While that's possible, you can increase your chances of an effective relationship with any one of these professionals if you engage in research before making your selection. Research is so much easier in these times of technological advancement, but it's also important to check more than one source, as a single source cannot always be relied upon. And as stated above, if you are deceived or taken advantage of, you know that you can withstand whatever consequences come from the deception of dishonesty and retain your self-dignity. The idea is to learn from the experience and ensure that in the future, the same "trust" error is not repeated. In this way, growth and development occurs.

Conversely, there is the trust we feel and have for those who are close to us – family, friends and close associates. This trust is built over years and many experiences – both the happy and sad occasions, the good times as well as the trials and tribulations. Trust that is tested constantly over the years will naturally be much stronger than the trust that is expected of us in the majority of life's situations. In this type of "developed" trust, one tends to feel comfortable and secure, and those who experience it feel comfortable in their relationships. If this type of trust is violated it can become life shattering. The person who trusted is, of course, devastated often to the point where s/he questions himself or herself, and their ability to ever trust again. In my research in distributing the questionnaires, one of the questions I asked was "if someone violated your trust, would you ever trust that person again?" It is significant to note that almost one-third of the respondents indicated that under no circumstances would they ever trust that person again. We learn over time that trust is fragile; it may take a long time to build it, but for some people, one major violation can eradicate a lifetime of building trust. So trusting others is about trusting yourself – that you can handle any violation of the trust that you put in others with calmness and dignity and that you don't "blindly" trust others but do your own research if and when necessary.

> "Only trust thyself, and another shall not betray thee."
> *-William Penn*
> *Founder of the Colony of Pennsylvania (1644–1718)*

You may wish to post your reflections or comments on www. trustontrial.com

Question: Think of a time when you trusted someone professionally.

Reflection: Did it work out well or were you disappointed? If disappointed, what, if anything, did you do about it? Was there a lesson to be learned?

Question: Can you think of a time when you had a "hunch" about trusting or distrusting someone or something?

Reflection: Did you go with your "hunch?" What was the result? If disappointed, how did you handle it?

PREMISE #3

Trust is about making a decision. One decides to trust.

"It's not hard to make decisions when you know
what your values are."
Roy Disney
Co-Founder of Walt Disney Company (1893–1971)

This appears to be a self-evident statement….or so it would seem. One of the respondents to a questionnaire indicated that he tended to rely on his "gut" feelings in trusting people and circumstances. He did not think of trusting his intuition as a decision but rather stated that it was a natural response that didn't involve a thinking process and that it was not a decision. I would advocate that it is a decision-making process made at the subconscious level effectively through a combination of experience, listening to one's instinct or intuition, and thinking through the situation. It's important to be aware of and realize that when trust is bestowed on someone, there is an internal decision being made, consciously or unconsciously, to allow this person to affect your life in some way, whether slightly or with great impact.

Trust cannot be just about going with our feelings if it is to be effective. Yes, there is much truth in "trusting your intuition," but we do this after gaining the understanding of what our intuition is and what it is telling us. Intuition is normally defined as a "keen and quick insight." Throughout our experiences we build a reservoir of knowledge or practical wisdom gained from what we have observed, encountered or undergone. We can think of our intuition as a "shortcut" that connects automatically to this knowledge or practical wisdom. Sometimes we are at a loss to explain why we just "know" something about which we feel strongly. When this happens, more than likely this "knowing" is our intuition kicking in. The 'keen and quick insight' can come out of nowhere and whether or not we trust it depends on how well we know ourselves and how well we trust ourselves (first two premises). After we've had many experiences with trusting this 'keen and quick insight' we are in a better position to interpret what it may mean to us and how to trust it. Understanding when the conditions are right for trusting and when more caution needs to be taken is very much a part of knowing yourself. After experience and intuition are well considered, the final analysis of whether to trust or not to trust becomes a decision we all must make. So even when one feels they just automatically trusted someone else, they really made a decision to trust at a subconscious level.

You may wish to post your reflections or comments on www. trustontrial.com

Question: **What was the last trust decision you made?**

Reflections: Did you make a quick decision to trust or did you really have to think it over? Did you know the person(s) involved very well? If an intuitional thought came quickly to your mind, did you ignore it or consider it? Did you feel comfortable with your decision to trust, once you made it? Why or why not?

PREMISE #4

Self-Confidence plays a major role in effective trust decisions.

"No one can make you feel inferior without your consent."
-Eleanor Roosevelt
First Lady of the United States (1884–1962)

This is yet another statement that seems self-evident; however, it merits further analysis. Of course, there is a strong connection to Premise #2...if one displays self-confidence then one is more likely to trust himself or herself and consequently more likely to make good decisions in trusting others. The premise implies that the better self-image one has, the more confidently one will create and pursue goals. Self-confidence can be defined as an awareness and belief in one's own potential. Therefore a lack of self-confidence can be described as an emphasis on one's limitations. A lack of self-confidence exhibits itself in many ways – shyness, timidity, guilt, anger, depression, self-doubt, paranoia, bragging, feelings of worthlessness, a false sense of humility, perfectionism, fear of change or making mistakes, and many more. People who suffer from paranoia will never make good "trust" decisions for they will trust no one, even when it would be important to trust a person or situation. There are many ways that people display a lack of self-confidence, such as being aggressive, being argumentative, engaging in negativity and self-deprecating statements and the like. The stronger one feels about one's own abilities, the better the decision-making process when deciding whom to trust or not to trust. And in relation to Premise #1, a person with self-confidence will quite likely be shaken if his/her trust is violated, but again will not lose control and cause harm in any way.

We automatically choose to trust others in certain situations such as driving or flying (as we discussed). Yes, we realize that our trust can be violated when drivers are drunk, not paying attention (talking on cell phones or, even worse, texting messages), or violating speeding ordinances which can result in disastrous consequences. However, we assess the situations we're in and make informed decisions as to whether we choose to drive or fly. The self-confident person will drive defensively at all times and do some research on the safest airlines before flying. However, we realize that accidents do happen and that we will handle whatever consequences might occur should we be the victim of an accident.

> "You may be deceived if you trust too much,
> but you will live in torment if you do not trust enough"
> *-Frank Crane*
> *American Film Stage Actor and Director (1873–1948)*

You may wish to post your reflections or comments on www. trustontrial.com

Question: Are you a self-confident person?

Reflections: How so? Have you always been self-confident? What actions have you engaged in that increased your self-confidence?

PREMISE #5

You, yourself, must be trustworthy in order to trust others and be trusted by them.

"Depend upon yourself. Make your judgment trustworthy by trusting it. You can develop good judgment as you do the muscles of your body – by judicious, daily exercise."
-Grantland Rice
American Writer (1880-1954)

If a person is known for being dishonest in their daily dealings with others then it stands to reason that in the passage of time this person will not be trusted by others. Honesty is a strong way to build trustworthiness and dishonesty is the quickest way to erode any trust that may have been built between two or more people. There is a truism about the concept of trust – that trust is earned and we must prove ourselves to be trustworthy in order to gain the trust and respect that we expect from others. But this gaining of trust and respect is achieved when one trusts and respects others. This is where the trust factors that we will be discussing come into play. Simply put, being honest, committed, sincere, dependable and reliable, fair, loyal and confident will indicate that you are trustworthy. Engaging in activities that suggest the opposite of these trust factors will in turn show you to be untrustworthy. The study of psychology reveals that human beings tend to project their own personal characteristics onto others. If you consider yourself trustworthy, you are more likely to trust others and others will be more likely to trust you. Conversely, if you are considered to be untrustworthy, you will be regarded with distrust. Abraham Maslow, a noted American psychologist, alerted us to the human need for security. When someone is trustworthy we tend to feel secure around them and again conversely, when we perceive someone to be untrustworthy we feel insecure in their presence. We have already addressed that trust is something that is earned over a period of time. True and important is the fact that trust is fragile. It is worth re-emphasizing here that while trust may take a long time to build, it can be broken with one major breach. Showing yourself to be trustworthy goes a long way in engendering trust from and in others.

You may wish to post your reflections or comments on www. trustontrial.com

<u>Question:</u>   How do you show yourself to be trustworthy?

<u>Reflections:</u>   Do you tend to trust others initially until your trust is broken? Do you tend to distrust until you come to realize that a person is trustworthy?

In beginning our exploration of the trust process, it is important that we consider these premises, as they shape the way that we "see" and experience trust. Their influence underlies the understanding of the trust factors and the application of these trust factors in our lives. Let us now take a look at these trust factors.

CHAPTER TWO

THE TRUST FACTORS

In this chapter we will explore the basics of trust – how we may define it and experience it. It is not my purpose to address the theoretical or pathological issues connected with trust or distrust but rather to simply examine the understanding of trust, the role it plays in our lives and what factors influence our own personal willingness to trust.

So what is this thing called trust? Have you asked yourself about your understanding of trust? If asked for your definition, would you be able to respond, and if so, how would you respond? What emotions or feelings do you experience when you trust or are trusted by someone? Or when you don't trust someone? Who are the people in your life that you trust implicitly? Are there any? If asked why you trust certain people over others, what would your response be?

These are questions that need answers, especially today as we tread the waters of transition in our rapidly changing world. On the other hand, it would appear that we have reached a point in history where many of our basic beliefs about the honesty and sincerity of people and events, both present and past, have been proven wrong, altered and/or discredited. Given the recent media reports of lying, cheating and stealing in businesses and organizations, governments, politics, religion and the real estate, finance, and mortgage industries, we realize that values have changed. Obviously, our ability to trust the "outside world" has been greatly affected by these recent events in our history. And so, the questions we've just asked ourselves about trust need to be explored and an understanding of trust developed so that we can be on more solid ground when the time comes for us to trust a person, situation or event.

As we begin this exploration, we keep in mind those premises that have been discussed in the previous chapter, especially the first premise which is "Know thyself." How many of us really do know who we are? Or why we act as we do? As logic would have it, if we don't really know who we are then, as Shakespeare suggested, we cannot be true to ourselves.

But first let us take a broader view of the concept of trust. As mentioned in the Introduction, my research began during my studies with the Crow Indians, whose understanding of trust is found in their translation of the word trust, which is "I believe in your word." The Native American understanding, when making an agreement or promise with someone, is that the agreement would last as long as the water flows and the grass grows. One of the results of this study is something that would seem obvious but in this world definitely bears repeating. As each of the members of both the Crow and Federal Government negotiating teams trusted themselves enough to take down their defense shields and truly come to know one another at a personal level, only then was any positive progress made in these negotiations. When the ability to truly identify with another person is exercised, then the possibilities for trust are opened. So personally, we have to leave the confines of our own private world and venture out into the world of others to understand their beliefs, hopes and desires and be open to their world while sharing our world of beliefs, hopes and desires. This is where the process of interpersonal trust starts.

At this point, we will examine each of the trust factors individually and 'think things through' for ourselves. The trust factors include: honesty, commitment, sincerity, dependability/reliability, loyalty, faith and confidence. Please remember that the first four trust factors were more overwhelmingly indicative of the respondents' responses (with a higher percentage of respondents naming these factors in the questionnaires) and that the remaining factors were mentioned less frequently.

HONESTY

"Honesty is such a lonely word, everyone is so untrue, honesty
is hardly ever heard, and mostly what I need from you."
-Billy Joel
American singer-songwriter (1949-   )

The first trust factor we will discuss is one that comes as no surprise, as without it, there can be no trust. If you look up the word "honesty" in the dictionary, you'll come across words like truthfulness and sincerity. Integrity, which usually is allied with the concept of honesty, differs somewhat in that it is defined as an adherence to moral principle and character – it deals primarily with being straightforward and frank. But if honesty is about being truthful then whose truth are we referring to? Some of us might feel that all situations are either black or white. However, many of us have encountered situations that appear to be more a reality of gray somewhere in between. Is there anyone reading this who has never told a lie? How do we distinguish in our own minds the difference between what we refer to as a "little white lie" and an out-and-out blatant damaging lie? How does one measure lies? Is telling a parent or spouse we were somewhere when we actually weren't as big a lie as telling the boss that we completed a project when we haven't? Where does one draw the line between a "big lie" and a "little lie?" Perhaps the words of Sir Walter Scott apply here – "Oh what a tangled web we weave when first we practice to deceive." Of course, we feel that upon dealing with someone who has been known to lie on more than one occasion, our reaction is to be less inclined to trust that person again. Paraphrasing another saying is this comment: "If you lie to me once, shame on you; if you lie to me twice, shame on me." Would this saying be implying that we shouldn't trust someone who lies twice? How many times does a person lie to us before we "decide" not to trust him/her? Obviously we are less likely to believe someone who is a repetitive liar. But the point at which we decide not to trust someone caught in many lies will be different for each of us and will depend on many factors, such as length of time we've known that person, the situation in which the trust relationship exists, the type of relationship involved, as well as other factors.

> "I'm not upset that you lied to me,
> I'm upset that from now on I can't believe you."
> *-Friedrich Nietzsche*
> *German philosopher (1844-1900)*

So why do people lie to begin with? What's the point in lying? The most basic motivator for lying is fear – fear of the consequences, fear of becoming vulnerable, fear of hurting someone's feelings or of appearing to be unkind, fear of losing a job, fear of losing an important person in our lives, and the list goes on. It is also true that fear can be a reason for telling the truth, such as fear of getting caught, fear of retaliation and so on. The main lesson to be learned here is that fear is a most powerful motivator – especially when it comes to dishonesty.

It's also important to realize that the role of lying in our own past experiences also shapes our ability to trust. If one is guilty of having lied significantly in the past, then that person is less likely to believe that someone else is telling the truth…and consequently less likely to trust others. It is also true that if a person has been deceived and/or betrayed often in one's life, that person also is less likely to trust others. As we are aware, in our society, women tend to know very little about cars and are therefore frequent victims of car repair scams. Therefore, women who have experienced being "ripped off" many times in the past are extremely skeptical of car repair shops. For this very reason, used car salesmen usually find themselves at the top of the 'least trusted' list. However, we find in recently conducted pools that those professions finding themselves at the bottom of today's "trust" lists include investment firms, mortgage companies, Wall Street and credit card companies. This is not a big surprise given our recent economic collapse.

So what does honesty look like in the home? As we grow, we are introduced to the concept of lying vs. truth telling in different ways. A child telling a falsehood in one family may be given a good "talking to" and punished accordingly, while in another family, the falsehood told by the child may be winked or chuckled at with no consequences. In yet a third family, the child's lie may be addressed sternly but still with no consequences. A different scenario might include the child telling similar untrue stories at various times but meeting with different reactions from authority figures (by authority figures we refer to parents, teachers, law enforcers, coaches, etc.) that range from authority ignoring the lie to inflicting various levels of consequences. We follow this child as he progresses to school and observes a classmate lying or engaging in dishonest acts and suffering no consequences from school authorities for the same actions for which s/he received serious consequences. Of course, confusion arises and a decision is reached by the child as to the what, how, when and why s/he will tell the truth or lie. Now our child has become an adult and enters the work world. S/he is introduced to an organizational culture where certain actions that were previously considered to be dishonest are now accepted business practices – such as tampering with or falsifying reports, not working the time required or not producing the work expected for the job. Yet another decision needs to be made by the adult. We see the unfolding of our premise that trust is a decision.

> "Integrity is telling myself the truth. And honesty
> is telling the truth to other people."
> *-Spencer Johnson*
> *American Author (1940-   )*

Finally, our understanding of honesty is shaped by the society in which we live. As we look at our present day society we see a country whose values are in the process of great change. In the past, we may have felt clear about the values we shared and those that we as a nation represented to the rest of the world...such values as freedom, independence and opportunity underlying our belief system and displayed on our money as "In God We Trust." It's safe to say that all of these values were founded on the basic concept of honesty. Yet we find our trust being violated almost daily by religious, federal, state and civil governmental institutions, and by business, political, and other leaders in every aspect of our lives.

Increasingly, in this last decade the departure from honesty in our dealings with each other has increased at an alarming rate. We hear constantly of identity theft, various scams before and after natural disasters as well as daily scams on the internet, citizens defrauding governmental programs meant for the poor and disadvantaged, etc. It is dishonesty that has led to the greatest real estate disaster ever perpetrated upon the American public to be followed by the collapse of the financial system…all a result of the greed and dishonesty of those we were led to believe we could trust. How can trust exist in this type of national environment? One wonders what one of our most revered presidents who gave his life to save the union of our country – "Honest Abe" – would think of the legacy he left us compared to the legacy we are now leaving our children?

"I desire so to conduct the affairs of this Administration that if at the end…I have lost every other friend on earth, I shall at least have one friend left, and that friend shall be down inside of me."
-Abraham Lincoln
16th President of the United States (1809-1865)

You may wish to post your reflections and/ or comments on www. trustontrial.com

Question: What are your perceptions regarding honesty?

Question: What have been your experiences with honesty?

Question: What did you agree or disagree with in this section on honesty and why?

Question: Do you have a favorite quote on honesty?

COMMITMENT

"Ya Gotta Wanna"

"Your depth of commitment, your quality of service, the product of
your devotion -- these are the things that count in life."
-Scott O'Grady
United States Air Force fighter pilot (1965-   )

While 'honesty' ranked the highest of the characteristics needed
for trust by respondents to the questionnaire, the second greatest
characteristic mentioned was the need for commitment in learning
to trust others. The dictionary definition of commitment is "to give
in trust or consign." Interesting that the word trust is used to define
the word commitment…we begin to realize how interrelated these
characteristics are to the concept of trust. A very simple definition of
commitment can be translated as "ya gotta wanna." Commitment
involves making a decision, emphasizing our premise that trust
is a decision. For some people making a commitment can be an
agonizing process. Obviously the level of the decision determines
the difficulty in making the decision. Making a decision to marry
someone with the accompanying understanding that the commitment
is for a lifetime goes far beyond making a decision as to what movie
to see on a given evening. Commitment also involves making a
pledge or promise to be or do something and to take responsibility
and accountability for that promise. Consequently, commitment
involves a certain amount of risk taking. And risk taking in turn
can imply a lack of security in the decision making process. What
do we find behind the inability to make commitments? Again, it is
fear! Fear of making a mistake, fear of being trapped by a decision
made long ago, fear of not having the energy or passion to supply
whatever is required by the person, project or process to whom the
commitment is being made. Should a commitment be broken, there
may be guilt, anger, blame, shame and other emotions experienced
by all parties involved in the commitment. This can be very
frightening. But the most often felt emotion when a commitment
is broken is that of betrayal, by both the person who broke the
commitment (this possibly at a subconscious level) as well as by the

person who is on the receiving end of the broken commitment. This occurs in personal relationships and in organizational situations as well. One of the major contributing factors to the anger displayed by many downsized employees in organizations today is the feeling of a broken commitment to the "cradle to grave" psychological work contract made between employer and employee many years ago. Because of the economic downturn brought on partly by global competition and the advancement of technology, many organizations chose to improve their bottom line by downsizing the organization. This downsizing phenomenon starting in the 1980's and continues to this day. Those employees affected by this downsizing in whatever form, experienced a sense of betrayal, rejection and abandonment by these organizations. These emotions that are experienced but not always expressed are most powerful, and all of us have read, heard and seen some of the effects these downsizings or firings have had on certain employees: depression, suicide and addiction to various substances (for those who expressed them internally) and violence towards others in the workplace (for those who expressed them externally).

Does commitment imply adhering to a pledge of promise made long ago that no longer serves the purpose or has become detrimental to one or all of the parties concerned? While a commitment may have been made in good faith at a certain point in time, circumstances and life situations do change over time and many events cannot be foreseen. Also, a commitment made between two people is made at a certain period in time, and over time these people grow, develop and change. Were these two people to make the same commitment after an extended period of time, they might not make the same commitment as they may be very different in their nature, thoughts and inclinations. So as these changes occur do the effects of the changes alter the commitment to some degree, possibly rendering the commitment null and void? Or is a commitment still a commitment regardless of the circumstances and ill effects? These are questions that are raised when a commitment is broken and must be examined and answered, particularly at the individual level and again at the family, community, social and national levels. It becomes clear that when making a commitment, clarity needs to be established as to the nature and extent of that commitment. Should time considerations enter into the commitment? Should quality, quantity, efficiency and effectiveness factors also be considered? These considerations are addressed in many business agreements/ commitments but not as often in personal commitments. Once again, since our society doesn't give much thought and consideration to these things, we then turn to our court systems to resolve these differences. In the institution of marriage, which certainly has experienced significant change in the past few decades, we have seen the growing use of prenuptial agreements. Are prenuptial agreements a necessity in our society? As we can see, commitment is a value that is definitely in the process of being altered and changed in our society. For those of us who would debate that a commitment is a commitment regardless of extenuating circumstances, we are left with the task of explaining the continuation of a commitment that has become harmful and detrimental to the parties involved. Is this the kind of commitment we wish for ourselves and our loved ones? Would it make common sense to remain in a present negative situation because of a commitment made in good faith many years before? Some may respond "yes" and others "no." For those of us who would debate that you change a commitment as the circumstances change, we are left with the task of clarifying who decides that the circumstances have changed enough to change the commitment. We must also face the necessity of how best to deal with the fallout that occurs as a result of the broken commitment, which can result in broken families and disorientation of a lifetime work. Our task remains to re-examine and re-evaluate the role of commitment in our understanding of trust.

"The relationship between commitment and doubt is by no means an antagonistic one. Commitment is healthiest when it is not without doubt but in spite of doubt."

-*Rollo May*
American Existentialist Psychologist (1909-1994)

You may wish to post your reflections and/ or comments on www. trustontrial.com

Question: What are your perceptions regarding commitment?

Question: What have been your experiences with commitment?

Question: What did you agree or disagree with in this section on commitment and why?

Question: Do you have a favorite quote on commitment?

SINCERITY

"Say what you mean and mean what you say!"
-Original Author unknown

If you've ever heard someone exclaim these words, you can be fairly sure that the tones of exasperation implicit in them have a lot to do with the topic of sincerity. They can be heard in conversations between husband and wife, parents and children, teachers and students, and employers and employees. Or perhaps you yourself have had the feeling when talking to someone, that they appeared to be giving you information you wanted to hear but something was missing. Maybe a certain sense of genuineness was lacking?

This characteristic was addressed often by the respondents to the questionnaire on trust. Upon reflection, it would make sense that sincerity, which the dictionary defines as a freedom from deceit, hypocrisy or duplicity, would have to be present in order for trust to exist. When we perceive someone as insincere we tend to feel some discomfort, the kind of discomfort that brings doubt to our minds about something that is being said or is taking place.

What might cause a person to insist that someone else say what they mean and mean what they say? No doubt, someone's past experience with a certain person has led them to realize that when this person expressed a certain sentiment, for example caring, friendship or support, they discovered later that it wasn't a genuine sentiment but rather something that seemed nice to say or do at the time or perhaps was the "easy way out," thereby showing a lack of sincerity. Why would anyone say something they didn't mean? There are many possible motivations involved in this situation: perhaps wanting to appear as a nice person but not interested enough in the situation, or wanting to show the other person that they care but not wanting to get involved, or even wanting to gain something from the situation for their own benefit with not much thought given to consequences; these are all reasons for not being sincere. Sincerity can at times feel somewhat ambiguous; however, everyone has a sense of when a person is being sincere or insincere. Sometimes there are visual clues as when the facial expression doesn't match what is being said. It is not something we are aware of consciously but perhaps subconsciously; even so, it can affect us to a large degree.

> "No man can produce great things who is not thoroughly
> sincere in dealing with himself"
> *-James Russell Lowell*
> *American Romantic poet and diplomat (1819-1891)*

The above quote addresses the need, as with honesty, to be sincere with ourselves. But also, as with honesty, it is difficult to be certain when we are being sincere in our motivations, and why we engage in certain words and acts with others. We may think on the surface that we are acting with the best of intentions, but were we to dig a little deeper we might discover we're using manipulation to have events or circumstances result in our favor.

This in and of itself is not duplicitous unless it results in what is absolutely good for us and not so good for the person being manipulated. Even if the action results in good possibilities for the manipulated person, it is insincere and therefore an untrustworthy action.

Today in organizations you will hear the phrase describing managers as "walking their talk." The basic meaning inherent in this phrase is that of sincerity. When management introduces the latest employee motivation program into an organization (or the "flavor of the month" as these programs are sometimes called) employees share a tendency to distrust the meaningfulness of the new program. This distrust is not related to the employees' unwillingness to be open to the new knowledge and skills being addressed but rather to a lack of belief in the management's sincerity. This doubt is due to past experiences with management. Often management turns to "gurus" for advice on encouraging employee participation in the administration of the organization's systems. However, when the employees' actual participation in the program causes the managers some discomfort, many of them tend to disregard or circumvent the original intent of these programs. The employees, who have invested much time, effort, skills and much hope into their work, then feel discouraged, betrayed and disgusted. Consequently, any similar programs that are introduced into the organization are met with distrust and suspicion.

So what does a healthy picture of sincerity look like? With sincerity we observe a sense of genuineness, frankness, candidness, straightforwardness and a certain guilelessness. When we are sincere, we do indeed say what we mean and mean what we say. There is no hidden agenda to deceive or mislead or portray something other than what it actually is. In treating people with sincerity and honesty, and in saying what you mean and meaning what you say, you become more trustworthy. Others who inevitably pick up on the sincerity, are more willing to trust. On the other hand, if a person appears sincere when sharing what they will do for you and you're aware through experience that they probably will not follow through, then it is their sincerity that comes into question. When detecting a lack of sincerity, one is much less likely to trust others. Regardless of appearance, actions do indeed speak louder than words.

> "So let us begin anew - remembering on both sides
> that civility is not a sign of weakness, and sincerity
> is always subject to proof."
> *John Fitzgerald Kennedy*
> *35th President of the United States (1917-1963)*

You may wish to post your reflections and/ or comments on www. trustontrial.com

Question: What are your perceptions regarding sincerity?

Question: What have been your experiences with sincerity?

Question: What did you agree or disagree with in this section on sincerity and why?

Question: Do you have a favorite quote on sincerity?

DEPENDABILITY/ RELIABILITY

"Do what you say you are going to do."

"You are already of consequence in the world if you are known as a man of strict integrity. If you can be absolutely relied upon; if when you say a thing is so, it is so; if when you say you will do a thing, you do it; then you carry with you a passport to universal esteem."

-Grenville Kleiser
American author (1868-1935)

It is not surprising that the respondents to the questionnaire on trust indicated dependability and reliability as essential to their need for trust. Dependability and reliability are often used interchangeably. The dictionary definition of dependability is "worthy of trust." This implies that we prove that we are worthy of another's trust - that we are trustworthy. Since trust is built over time, as we continue to do what we say we are going to do then we show ourselves to be dependable. Reliability means following through on our commitments, as we have just mentioned, and doing what we say we will do. When we are reliable, others can count on us, and we can count on ourselves.

We are reminded by the elder generation that there was a time in our country when "a man's word was his honor." An agreement was sealed with a handshake and both parties expected and relied upon the other one to deliver on the agreement. Apparently, there was actually a time in our history when one didn't enter into an agreement armed with all kinds of legal papers, tools and "whatnots" and "wherefores." We can only assume, given the legal entanglements we find ourselves in today, that there must have been many unreliable and undependable people who appeared on the scene along the way, and, after many broken agreements and much anger and betrayal, changed the course of how we do business and enter into relationships today.

In the workplace this lack of dependability and reliability displays itself in what is referred to as a lack of cooperation. When two people or two departments must work with each other to develop a product or complete a project and one of them is seen as unreliable, the nature of the work relationship is affected adversely. A tone of cautiousness persists, finger pointing spreads and a negative work environment begins to be established. Obviously, this work environment does not promote the quality of product and service that most organizations strive for as stated in their mission and vision statements. Lack of dependability can create deep fissures of suspicion in all kinds of relationships, some which will never be corrected and repaired enough to re-establish a full sense of trust.

"The obvious advantage is the trust, loyalty and dependability that you have from and for your customers, employees, suppliers and stockholders."

-Dan Rottenberg
American author, editor, journalist

There are people in our lives whom we may not like personally but because they have proven themselves to be dependable, they have nevertheless earned our trust. Our past experiences with the issues of dependability and reliability will determine to a large degree how dependable we see ourselves and others. Lack of dependability from others can take a tremendous toll on the psyche in all areas of life.

Understanding reliability and dependability can start with your own sense of who you are and how you define dependability for yourself. Once this is clear, another area up for inspection is how you apply this same definition to others in your life. Occasionally we come across people who have one definition of dependability for themselves but apply a different and more stringent version of dependability for others. Of course, this can be said for all eight trust factors that we are addressing. However, dependability is an area where it seems to have more impact. Once we know these things about ourselves, we are in a better position to decide which of the people in our lives we can depend upon and more importantly why it is that we do depend upon them. This knowledge can help us define for ourselves what trust is and how we use it in our daily lives.

"The shifts of fortune test the reliability of friends."
-Marcus Cicero
Roman philosopher (106BC-46BC)

You may wish to post your reflections and/ or comments on www. trustontrial.com

Question: What are your perceptions regarding dependability/ reliability?

Question: What have been your experiences with dependability/ reliability?

Question: What did you agree or disagree with in this section on dependability/reliability and why?

Question: Do you have a favorite quote on dependability/ reliability?

FAIRNESS

"Fairness is what justice really is."
-Potter Stewart
Associate Justice of the US Supreme Court (1915-1985)

Fairness is a characteristic that respondents to the questionnaires frequently used to describe trust. The dictionary definition includes words such as: 'free from bias,' 'dishonesty,' and 'injustice.' Fairness as a characteristic is complex as it can be very subjective – that is, what may seem to be fair to one individual may be perceived as unfair to another. The question can become – to whose truth or sense of fairness do we defer? The context in which something is deemed to be fair or unfair plays a crucial role. In most cases, treating everyone fairly does not mean treating them alike.

Our legal courts are filled with dockets of cases where individuals are on opposite sides of an issue – with both sides seeing their position as the right, true and fair one. One of the popular shows on television involves the airing of actual court cases that are discussed in front of a judge who renders a final decision. Following the decision, interviews are held with both parties who are then questioned about the judge's decision. The defendant and plaintiff will of course agree or disagree with the decision depending upon whether they feel they were favored or discriminated against. Since fairness is based to a large degree on values, our personal values may differ significantly from the values on which a court bases its decisions – so is this fair? Also, because of the accumulation of laws over almost two hundred years, some of them archaic or left unrevised, justice or fairness may not prevail in favor of adherence to the letter of the law. As an aside, it is interesting to note that in our society equality is often equated with fairness, when in fact to treat all parties involved equally may not ultimately be the fair thing to do.

There can be and are enough similarities of backgrounds and experiences in our country to discuss a general sense of what it is to be fair at home, at play, at school and at work. Some examples of perceived fairness or unfairness include: in the home, when there is discussion regarding fair and equitable duties shared by partners and children; at school, when there is an attempt to ensure that all students, regardless of sex, age, physical ability or belief systems, receive an equal opportunity to obtain a good education; in recreation, when there is the inclusion of technology in football games, for example, of the "instant replay" to assist the referees who were appointed to ensure that the game is being played fairly. And at work, where perhaps this fairness attempt is felt the strongest, there has been the inclusion of much legislation to ensure that employees are dealt with fairly from the perspectives of job promotion, accessibility, opportunity for training and many other work issues.

Sometimes in an attempt to make things fair in the workplace, employees are surveyed to obtain their impressions as to whether some of the existing human resource policies are fair (of course, some of them are mandated by law). Then giving weight to the responses of the survey, policies are adjusted accordingly. The question remains – is this fair? Some employees would absolutely agree that this is the best way to achieve fairness in the workplace and some employees would strongly object to this method, as not all employees find themselves in the same circumstances, and addressing only the majority's opinion is unfair. So who's right? Whose perception of reality is right and is there really a best, right and only way to establish fairness in the workplace?

So what does a healthy picture of fairness look like? Again, the characteristic of fairness is one of the most complicated factors we are dealing with in this look at trust. It is determined primarily by a person's values, experiences and perceptions. So what do you think is fair? Fairness as we can see, is in the eye of the beholder. As long as there are differing perceptions of the same situation, the question of fairness will always be disputed and never resolved to everyone's satisfaction.

"Expecting the world to treat you fairly because you are a good person is a little like expecting the bull not to attack you because you are a vegetarian."

Dennis Wholey
American television host and producer (1939-)

You may wish to post your reflections and/ or comments on www. trustontrial.com

Question: What are your perceptions regarding fairness?

Question: What have been your experiences with fairness?

Question: What did you agree or disagree with in this section on fairness and why?

Question: Do you have a favorite quote on fairness?

LOYALTY

"When we are debating an issue,
loyalty means giving me your honest
opinion, whether you think I'll like it or not.
Disagreement, at this state,
stimulates me. But once a decision is made,
the debate ends. From that
point on, loyalty means executing
the decision as if it were your own."

-Colin Powell
American statesman,
retired 4-star general and Secretary of State (1937-)

Another factor in our examination of trust is that of loyalty. When conducting the follow-up interviews to discover more about what respondents to the questionnaires meant when stating loyalty as a factor for trust, their responses pointed in the direction of a combination of commitment, consistency and faithfulness. The dictionary defines loyalty as faithfulness to commitments or obligations. How then does this differ from dependability? Given this definition and the respondents' clarification of their answers, it appeared that loyalty is seen as the ability to commit and persevere in reaching a goal or following a leader for a specified period of time. We've all heard the expression of "fair weather fans" as applied to professional sports, indicating that the sports fans will support their team only as long as the team is winning. Well, loyalty for the respondents indicated a sense of "stick-to-it-ivity." So we could say that loyalty is <u>not</u> sticking to a commitment of a goal, a leader or an issue only when things are going well. Loyalty implies staying committed through thick and thin.

In families, perhaps this sense of loyalty is generally stronger as is understood in the expression "blood is thicker than water." There is a certain bonding and a closeness that exists between family members, an understanding that occurs even without words being spoken. An outsider may observe much quarreling and infighting among the family members but whenever an external threat is perceived, these family members will defend each other to the death if necessary. This kind of loyalty tends to be greatly admired in our society although it does have its negative side. Family members can enable each other in bad situations when a more confrontative rather than loyal approach is needed. In addition, this perceived loyalty has been rapidly eroding these past few decades. We have all heard of families where members have not acknowledged or spoken to each other for years over a perceived or actual hurt or injustice. The individuals involved continue to nurture their hurt and resentment rather than muster up the courage to approach each other to resolve their differences and strengthen the ties that bind them. Our sense of loyalty is indeed changing.

In organizations, the downsizing evidenced in today's workforce these past few decades has contributed to the eroding of the loyalty factor that existed in the past. Prior to the 1980's, the psychological work contract that existed was that management would guarantee a job, decent salary and good work conditions and the employee would follow the rules of the workplace and perform their work effectively. We have already mentioned the effects that downsizing has had on the commitment and sincerity trust factors. The loyalty factor has been greatly affected by these downsizings, restructurings or rightsizings as they are sometimes referred to. With these downsizings, employees felt betrayed, rejected and abandoned; perhaps, even insulted as the salaries of top officials skyrocketed (American executives enjoy the highest salaries of executives in the same fields throughout the world) as the employees were being ushered out of their jobs and left to fend for themselves to pursue their livelihood elsewhere.

> "You've got to give loyalty down, if you want loyalty up."
> *-Donald T. Regan*
> *66th US Secretary of the Treasury (1918-2003)*

What does a healthy picture of loyalty look like? Loyalty implies faithfulness; to one's word, to one's commitment and obligations, and to one's allegiances. Loyalty does also implies a timely purposefulness and dedication to a committed goal or a group of people. When it becomes obvious that the relationship has grown unhealthy for one and for all, and the sense of loyalty is withdrawn, loyalty may then take the shape of not doing anything that would dishonor the former allegiance. A healthy picture of loyalty looks like a commitment to a cause or relationship or group that one truly believes in, while retaining the ability to withdraw from that commitment if it should change, and move on with grace and dignity to rededicate oneself to another cause that one has grown into.

You may wish to post your reflections and/ or comments on www. trustontrial.com

Question: What are your perceptions regarding loyalty?

Question: What have been your experiences with loyalty?

Question: What did you agree or disagree with in this section on loyalty and why?

Question: Do you have a favorite quote on loyalty?

FAITH/CONFIDENCE

"Without faith, nothing is possible. With it, nothing is impossible."
-Mary McLeod Bethune
American Educator and Civil Rights Leader (1875-1955)

"If you once forfeit the confidence of
your fellow citizens, you can never
regain their respect and esteem. It is true that
you may fool all of the people
some of the time; you can even fool some of the
people all of the time; but
you can't fool all of the people all of the time."
-Abraham Lincoln
16th President of the United States (1809-1865)

We close our discussion on the trust factors with a look at the belief and faith factors. These last two trust factors will be addressed together as they imply similar meanings, and were mentioned less frequently than the other trust factors in the questionnaires. For instance, having faith or believing in the leader of an organization or one's manager or supervisor also implies having confidence in their knowledge, skills and abilities. There are some leaders and managers who are so charismatic that followers find themselves willing to believe in them merely because of their charisma. However, there are some leaders and managers who have earned our trust because of their role modeling of behaviors that inspire trust such as has been discussed. These factors of belief and confidence are more nebulous in nature. They imply a kind of gut feeling – our intuition kicks in, our built-in antennae pick up intangible clues, and our body systems react favorably or unfavorably as the case may be. With faith and confidence we learn to come to trust ourselves and our own intuition. Conversely, when our belief and faith in someone is violated, we begin to question ourselves – our values, our understanding of who we are, our ability to reason effectively.

Cecile T. Massé, Ph.D.

"Faith is a passionate intuition."
-William Wordsworth
English Romantic poet (1770-1850)

Faith is defined as confidence and trust in someone or something. Again we see how closely aligned our trust factors are as two of these trust factors are used to define this one concept of faith. Faith is a very personal attribute in the sense that it is a belief that is not based on proof yet is used to address a system of belief, or the understanding of obligation of loyalty to certain people, causes and events. As a reminder of my research conducted with the Crow Indians, their word for trust translated is "I believe in your word." The word 'believe' is a crucial part of their definition. Belief is defined as a confidence in the truth or existence of something not immediately susceptible to rigorous proof. Consequently, belief implies that though there may be no proof or tangible evidence through the laws of physics or other sciences, the believer is motivated to pursue credibility in someone or something through an inner knowing which cannot be explained. Oftentimes, the word belief is used in reference to a deity, a supreme being, a creator and ruler of the universe. All cultures carry their own mythologies and belief systems. We come to realize how endemic belief is to the whole process of trust.

Because there is no proof required in the belief system, it becomes easier to manipulate the system toward the acceptance of a few leaders' understanding and motivation toward more personal desires rather than the good of the religious community. As we research the effects of religion on people we find many good and wonderful actions as well as many dark and evil actions. There have been many religious organizations that have experienced lying, cheating and stealing by their religious leaders in the past few decades. People who have been duped by religious leaders have had their trust broken severely. Therefore, our experience can lead us to suspect someone or a group of people who profess a strong belief in someone or something. We have come to realize that while it is true that a belief can lead someone to accomplish extraordinary things, it is also true that this same strong belief can lead people to violate others' accepted ethical standards or belief systems. Consider the "Holy Wars" between the Catholics and Protestants in Ireland and the religious differences between the Arabs and Israelites. As Americans, we ourselves have participated in wars with Iraq over ethical and religious beliefs and are even now engaged in wars in Afghanistan. Or consider another volatile issue in our society today – that of abortion. We have been made aware of the case of the man who was so impassioned by his belief against abortion that he willingly and admittedly killed a doctor who was performing legalized abortions. The contradiction of his action versus his belief system suggests that the murder was not really about a belief system but more likely was a desire to inflict his personal motivation on another human being. In this case, a person who claims to believe in the sacredness of life violates this very belief by taking the life of someone who doesn't share his belief system. The hypocrisy in the action is readily apparent. We have to ask ourselves, what is wrong with this picture? There can be irrational actions committed by a people who hold strong beliefs and whose intention is to force their belief system on others who do not share that belief. Again, most of the wars going on at this very point in time confirm this statement. And again, we have to ask ourselves, what is wrong with this picture? Particularly with the faith/confidence trust factor do we have to employ critical thinking skills, emotional intelligence and the Triple A approach to be addressed in the last chapter.

You may wish to post your reflections and/ or comments on www. trustontrial.com

Question: What are your perceptions regarding faith/confidence?

Question: What have been your experiences with faith/confidence?

Question: What did you agree or disagree with in this section on faith/confidence and why?

Question: Do you have a favorite quote on faith/confidence?

We have discussed the eight factors that play a major role in the trust relationship. The purpose of this book is to encourage readers to understand which of these factors play the larger role in their ability to trust others, events and situations. We will now look at these trust factors in three major arenas of our lives – an intrapersonal look at trust, a look at trust as seen in our families, and finally a discussion of the trust relationship in organizations.

CHAPTER THREE

A PERSONAL LOOK AT TRUST

At this point, in looking at the formation of trust – the factors that comprise it and the role that these factors play in our ability and willingness to trust – we do so with the intention of looking at how we as individuals deal with trust on a daily basis. In doing so, our success in being honest with ourselves will determine how well this exploration develops.

As a point of review, the 8 trust characteristics that we explored are: honesty, commitment, sincerity, dependability/reliability, fairness, loyalty, and faith/confidence. The role that these characteristics play in the trusting process was discussed from the perspective of how they are displayed and expressed in today's society. We will now look at the role each of these characteristics plays in our personal understanding of trust.

First, we ask the question: why trust at all? Psychologists tell us through their research that basic trust is the cornerstone of a vital personality. It would seem obvious to us that trust is crucial in the context of our daily lives. Without it, our families, organizations and societies would be in chaos and upheaval. If we were to be constantly distrustful, fearful and suspicious of everyone in our lives, all activity would come to a halt – we would be facing paralysis. It is critical for us to employ a trusting attitude, not only from a healthy productive perspective but also from a healthy mental, psychological and spiritual perspective. Our survival, growth and development needs require that we employ trust to some level. The decision is not whether we trust or not trust but rather to what degree do we choose to trust. Given that we must trust to survive, it is important that we look at the different levels of trusting.

There are three basic levels to be addressed: the individual level, the family level and the organizational/societal level. At this point we will take an in-depth view of the individual level. One's ability to trust at a personal level begins with our introduction to this concept at the beginning of our life on this earth. Our early childhood experiences will determine to a large degree our initial preferences to trust or not trust.

TRUSTING OURSELVES

In the first chapter we addressed a basic trust premise: trusting others is about trusting ourselves. So let's take a look at some indicators that can help you see if and how you trust yourself. In your basic approach to trust, how would you answer this question: Do you automatically trust someone until they violate your trust in some way? Or do you automatically not trust someone until they prove that they are trustworthy? For most of us, we approach others with a "yes" response to both these questions in varying degrees and for various situations. However, for each of us there is most likely a tendency to go one way or the other. Is there a right, best and only way to approach this question? Certainly not. However, my point is to be aware of your own personal pattern to initially trust or distrust. Most likely, your response will provide insight about who you trust or don't trust and why.

You may wish to post your reflections or comments on www.trustontrial.com

Question: What is your basic reaction to trust?

Reflections: Do you instinctively trust someone upon meeting him/her? Do you rely upon your intuition when you choose to trust or not to trust upon meeting someone? Which reaction tends to predominate?

Question: Can you think of a time when you had a "hunch" about trusting or distrusting someone or something?

Reflection: Did you go with your "hunch?" What was the result? If disappointed, how did you handle it?

SELF-ESTEEM

In trusting ourselves, we are dealing with our sense of self-esteem. There are so many books and discussions on self-esteem that it is not my intent here to address self-esteem in depth. It is true that our sense of self-esteem is a major basic driving force behind many of our actions and can determine to a large degree what we do or don't accomplish in our lives. It is closely tied in to other related concepts such as self-approval, self-value, self-care and so forth. A sound definition of self-esteem would constitute "a realistic respect for or favorable impression of oneself." Having healthy self-esteem would include respecting oneself and displaying confidence in one's abilities. The opposite of self-esteem would be self-deprecation, where the person frequently makes negative "I am" statements, and tends to emphasize one's failings and weaknesses. This person expresses a strong need to please others in lieu of expressing confidence in his/her own beliefs, thoughts. Being on the defensive (doing such things as putting others down, avoiding accountability for actions, and being critical of others and yet overly sensitive to criticism) can also connote symptoms of lack of self-esteem such as.

As children, the responses obtained from our parents, church, school and community also contribute to what we believe about ourselves early in life. Some parents praised their children in their accomplishments and others spared their children praise in the hopes of keeping them humble. Some teachers favored the smart children in the classroom as opposed to those who struggled to learn. Classmates and community members may have admired and appreciated those children who were athletically gifted and ignored those who were not. Our self-esteem was also formed in the comparison to those around us.

It is important to realize that trusting yourself is closely tied into how you feel about yourself, and that includes how valued you feel and how powerful or powerless you see yourself. So we now know that self-esteem plays a major role in our willingness to trust ourselves.

You may wish to post your reflections or comments on www.trustontrial.com

Question: What were you taught about trust as a child?

<u>Reflections:</u>   Were you raised in a trusting family environment? What factors encouraged or discouraged trust in your family environment?

Question: What profession are you in?

<u>Reflections:</u>   Did you select it? Are you happy in your work life? Why or why not?

VALUES

Another major player in this area is the role played by values. A value can be defined as a principle or quality intrinsically seen as desirable. Our background experiences and beliefs shape the values that we hold dear today. Values were instilled into us at an early age. If childhood consisted of a close family situation where parents, extended family members and neighbors were also friends, then the value of family will be stronger in our adult years than if any or all these situations were lacking during childhood. If parents were close and supportive to their children in their childhood as opposed to parents who were distant and non-demonstrative, the value of close parenting will be strong. This feedback formed our understanding of values that were important in the world around us.

We now see how closely both self-esteem and values impact our self-image and consequently our "place in the world." Again, experts tell us that our values are fairly constant in our lives but do change when we experience what is referred to as a "significant emotional event." This event can be something dramatic or traumatic in our lives such as a death, divorce, an accident, health issues or the like. However, our values can also be changed by something less traumatic such as reading a book, seeing a movie or attending a meeting or class that greatly affects us and allows us to see things differently, thereby changing our values in some way. Again, our values do indeed affect our willingness to trust. As we meet other people who share our same values, be they the same religious belief system, the same station in life, the same political belief, the same occupation, the same skin color, or the same sexual orientation, we are more willing to trust them because there is something that is shared in common with these individuals. Consequently, to the degree that people are different from the way we are, we are less inclined to trust them. This "difference" can lead to great distrust, and as we have seen recently in our society it can also lead to hate and violence. If we perceive people as "different" from us and our belief systems, such as in sexual orientation, nationality or various religious beliefs, we tend to distrust them. One of the outcomes of my research with the Crow Indians and the Federal Government, as mentioned previously in the book, is that trust can be increased significantly with the willingness to be open to getting to know the person who is distrusted, and learning and understanding the "how" and "why" behind these differences.

> "You can't shake hands with a clenched fist."
> *-Indira Ghandhi*
> *Prime Minister of the Republic of India (1917-1984)*

At this point, let's review some of the major points we are making about personal trust. First, trust is the cornerstone of a vital, healthy personality and is essential to our survival. Second, in trusting at the personal level, we know that self-esteem and values play a major role in understanding how we trust ourselves. With this in mind, let's now move on to a question that we can ask ourselves to further understand our willingness to trust.

CHARACTERISTICS DEFINING TRUST/DISTRUST

In the questionnaire distributed to respondents during my research on trust, one of the questions asked was: "What words would you use to describe how you feel when you trust others?" I would encourage readers to answer this question for themselves before reading on. The respondents answered this question with words like comfortable, supported, acknowledged, affirmed, loved, serene, worthy, respectable, encouraged, approved and inspired. Obviously, these are all positive words reflecting a sense of not only untroubled conditions but providing a sense of peace and acceptance in the recipient. It would follow that attempting to build trust both within oneself and with others would include creating an environment reflecting the flavor of these words. Additionally, knowing how many of these descriptors you experience when you trust someone is equally important. So why do you trust a person? What actions does s/he engage in that cause you to feel positive? While we would expect the answer to this question to be the same for all of us, there most probably would be different answers for each of us because our own unique self-esteem and value systems, backgrounds, experiences and beliefs are different.

Another question on the distributed questionnaire included the opposite of the first question, and that is: "What words would you use to describe how you feel when you don't trust someone?" Again, how would you answer this question? Responses to this particular question included: angry, fearful, annoyed, deceived, suspicious, disgusted, dislike, apprehension, alarmed, intimidated, uneasy, irritated, disturbed, as well as several others. Again, one doesn't have to be a rocket scientist to determine that these words convey an environment of fear and distaste. Are there any people in your life whose presence brings up a sense of these descriptions? Obviously, it would be safe to say that these are people you tend to distrust. Again, in what actions do they engage that evoke those negative feelings in you? Are these people merely different or have they violated your trust at some point in time? Could they do anything to regain your trust?

This brings us to yet another question in the same questionnaire. The results of this particular question were somewhat surprising. The question was: "If someone violated your trust would you trust them again?" I projected that about 15 to 20% of the respondents would say "no." However, the actual results indicated that 33% or one-third of the respondents indicated that "no, they would never trust them again." This would indicate that the level of distrust in our society might be quite higher than we think. Of the two-thirds who responded that "yes" they would trust them again, the following question remained, and that was: "what would it take for you to trust them again?" (This is a question our political, business, financial, religious and governmental leaders should be asking themselves!!). Respondents answered: 1) an apology is required, 2) a promise to never again violate one's trust is crucial, as well as 3) a demonstration, or several demonstrations in the future, that the violation will never be repeated. The preceding results were followed by other various answers addressing similar demands or all of these demands. How would you, the reader, have responded to this question? Are you willing to trust someone again who has violated your trust in any way? What would you expect them to do to regain your trust? The response to this question can shed some light on your relationship to trust issues as well as the person who is distrusted.

Understanding one's own personal relationship to trust issues is obviously a starting point in continuing on this adventure of discussing and understanding trust in families and in the work environment. Obtaining a solid foundation in one's own perception of trust can lead to being aware of changes in trust as they occur in one's life, and being prepared to deal with these changes effectively.

At this point, we can walk through the individual's relationship to the trust factors as addressed in the previous chapter and offer some guidance on how to apply them in one's own personal understanding of trust.

***You may wish to post your reflections or comments on www.
trustontrial.com***

Question: What words would you use to describe how you feel
                   when you trust someone?

Question: What words would you use to describe how you feel
                   when you don't trust someone?

Question: If someone violated your trust would you trust them
                   again? If so, what would they have to do to regain
                   your trust?

<u>Reflections</u>:   What thoughts came to your mind as you were
                   answering these questions?

HONESTY

The first descriptor of trust relates to honesty. It's safe to say
that without honesty, trust cannot exist. But what is your definition
of honesty? Again in the previous chapter we talked about "little
white lies" not really being counted by most of us as a violation
of honesty. As we discussed, sometimes little white lies are to
prevent someone else's feelings from getting hurt or to keep us out
of trouble (which is why, of course, most lies are told.) At work,
we sometimes take things that don't belong to us and which we
figure are inconsequential, ranging from office supplies to tools
and sometimes to equipment. We rationalize that these items won't
be missed or that we deserve them. The problem of course is that
these actions of stealing tend to build up to bigger actions of stealing
and we find ourselves engaging in significant acts of stealing or
dishonesty in general. While very few of us may have engaged in
embezzlement or larceny, it is important to remember that these acts
grow out of "insignificant" rationalizations. Oftentimes we hear
when persons are caught embezzling, that the perpetrators explain
they started with stealing smaller amounts without getting caught.
They found it was easy and continued to embezzle with the amounts
growing larger and larger over time. Their rationalization is always

that they assumed that they would never get caught. In the news, we have seen criminals apprehended for lying, cheating and stealing, believing that they would never get caught. Bernie Madoff, a prominent investment manager, created the largest financial scam in Wall Street history. He defrauded thousands of investors of billions of dollars. In confessing to his sons, he admitted that his whole business was just "one big lie." I guess we could all agree that this falls into the category of big lies!! There have been so many stories of embczzlement discovered recently in businesses, churches, and even city and federal governments. The "excitement" of the danger in possibly being caught brings on the adrenaline, and the embezzler becomes addicted to the act almost more so for the thrill of it than for the money itself. Lying and cheating fall into the same category as stealing or embezzling. The frequency of lies can become overwhelming. People who lie frequently, and are oftentimes caught in the lie, discover that they create a maelstrom for themselves. They come to recognize that they are indeed no longer trusted because of these lies. A recently released movie entitled "The Invention of Lying" addressed this very theme. It related the situation of a young man who lived in an alternate reality where lying was unknown… everyone tells the truth and only the truth. The story revolves around this young man who discovered the concept of lying and began to take advantage of those around him who only knew how to tell the truth. This advantage rocketed him to fame and fortune. However, he came to learn of the downside of lying and how dishonesty can reap unwanted disastrous consequences and he loses the one person who means the most to him.

Knowing that you're not trusted by others can be defeating in and of itself. What about keeping secrets? Is it acceptable to keep secrets? Where does this range on your personal honesty scale? Is it fine with you to keep secrets or is it a form of dishonesty? Secrets, out of necessity, very often lead to lies which necessitate more lies, until situations become overwhelming and out of control. It's important to remember that the more we try to project an image that is not who or what we are, the more we get caught up in our own deceptions. Another perspective on this topic is the ability to be honest with ourselves. It's been said that the most difficult thing we can ever do in our lives is to be honest with ourselves...but it's well worth the effort!

You may wish to post your reflections or comments on www. trustontrial.com

Question: How do you feel about lying?

Reflection: Do you differentiate between "big" and "little" lies? Have you ever gotten caught in a lie? Did it change your perspective about lying? How do you feel about secrets? Would you agree that secrets are a form of lying? Why or why not?

COMMITMENT

Commitment, as we've discussed, can go a long way in developing trust in ourselves and others. For example, we can be enthusiastic about a certain event or experience in our life and make a commitment to it. Our intentions are good; however, after a period of time, our interest dwindles and consequently, so does our commitment. What does one do in this situation to ensure that trust is developed? Being aware and alert to our fading enthusiasm and commitment is the first step to be taken. Deciding whether or not we want to recommit is the next decision to be made. If the decision leans towards breaking the commitment, then an honest communication of the decision to disengage from the people involved is crucial. Commitment is all about "ya gotta wanna" and if the "wanna" is no longer present, then honesty with yourself and with others is what is called for in building and maintaining trust. What if the original commitment was made for a lifetime? Does one stay committed forever? Or does one come to the realization that the commitment can no longer stand? These are decisions that have to be thought through and followed through with effective communication.

You may wish to post your reflections or comments on www. trustontrial.com

Question: Have you ever made a commitment that you needed to break?

Reflection: If so, what did you eventually do? How did you handle it? Would you make the same decision today if you had it to do over? Why or why not?

SINCERITY

What of your relationship to the descriptor of sincerity? We all understand and realize the importance to "say what you mean and mean what you say." Insincerity is probably the greatest killer of trust after honesty as it gives rise to feelings of abandonment, rejection and anger to the recipients of the insincere action. The message it sends is that of "I can't be bothered so I'll just tell you what you want to hear and do what I feel like doing." To have someone treat you with insincerity can feel demeaning and devaluing. At work, insincerity can demonstrate itself as a boss asking you about your family, knowing that s/he's doing it because the management principles indicate that it's the thing to do and not because the boss is sincerely interested.

You may wish to post your reflections or comments on www. trustontrial.com

Question: Have you ever been treated with insincerity?

Reflection: If so, what was your reaction? Did your feeling toward the person(s) who committed the insincere act change? If so, how so?

DEPENDABILITY/RELIABILITY

The maxim of "say what you mean and mean what you say" also applies to this trust factor. When you tell someone that you'll do something or be somewhere for them at a certain time and are significantly late, or worse still – don't show up at all, the results will produce anger, abandonment and frustration on the part of the person(s) who found you to be unreliable. Dependability plays a larger role at home, at work and at play when the realization exists that a partner, co-worker or team member cannot be relied upon. Once someone is perceived as unreliable, the trust level is greatly diluted and it is a long journey back to re-establishing trust. The journey is made longer when someone is perceived as being dishonest as well.

You may wish to post your reflections or comments on www. trustontrial.com

Question: Have you ever broken your word in agreeing to support someone?

Reflection: How did you feel after breaking your word? How did the other person feel?

LOYALTY

Loyalty is also a trust factor that depends upon the people and the situation involved. It is probably best understood by looking at its opposite, which is disloyalty and treachery. When we enter into an agreement or deal of any kind with the intent of not following through, this is indeed deceit and duplicity. As a personal trust factor, loyalty implies supporting a cause or situation with the utmost dedication. We probably can all identify with a loyal sports fan, sticking with the favored team through thick and thin. However, there are instances where loyalty may be a detriment as opposed to a support. Whether it's to a marriage, a good cause or an organization, loyalty may not be what's needed as indicated in the phrase "misplaced loyalty." Knowing whether to move on or stay, and making the decision as to when to move on and when to stay can be excruciatingly difficult. The best guidance in this situation is to be clear and honest with yourself and others stating (in an appropriate and timely manner), when and why the need for loyalty has been changed.

You may wish to post your reflections or comments on www. trustontrial.com

Question: How do you feel about the loyalty trust factor?

<u>Reflection:</u>   Is it important? Have you ever been disloyal? Can disloyalty be justified? Why or why not?

FAIRNESS

As discussed, fairness is a more difficult factor to deal with, as there are as many perspectives on fairness as there are people involved in an "unfair" situation. However, there can be instances when the violation of fairness is blatant and unmistakable. One way to determine whether actions taken will be perceived as fair or not is to actually check with the people whom the decision or action will impact the most. This action serves as an opportunity to detect weaknesses in the decision to be made concerning fairness. Fairness always implies approaching a decision with the idea of achieving justice and impartiality to the extent that this is actually possible.

You may wish to post your reflections or comments on www. trustontrial.com

Question: How would you describe fairness?

<u>Reflection:</u>   Have you been in a situation where you thought something was fair or unfair, yet other people saw it differently? What was your reaction?

FAITH/CONFIDENCE

Faith and belief play a most significant role in our ability to trust when we focus this factor on ourselves. Believing in oneself brings the greatest benefit in developing our ability to trust others. Believing in ourselves heightens our ability to believe in others. Trust definitely implies a faith; however, you'll need to define for yourself how faith and belief display themselves in your life. Always looking to others to supply your answers and your understanding because you "believe" in them can bring confusion and negative results in your life.

Confidence directly relates to our discussion of self-esteem in the previous chapter. It is crucial to be aware that having confidence in oneself is the beginning of trust. In gaining confidence in your abilities and talents, you are then in a much better position to place your confidence in others who resonate the same characteristics and qualities that prove to be trustworthy. Confidence is really what trust is all about.

You may wish to post your reflections or comments on www. trustontrial.com

Question: What are your perspectives on faith and confidence as trust factors?

Reflection: Do you have any examples where faith and confidence affected you to a great degree?

In our personal look at trust, we begin to realize that trusting others is really about trusting ourselves. Learning to trust is a process; it happens and evolves over time. Trust is also cyclical in that you are never really there. Sometimes in our quest to know ourselves and consequently trust ourselves, we find that we may take giant steps or little steps on our journey. Your experiences on this journey to trust may be exhilarating or disappointing, but nevertheless they are changing and shaping your willingness to trust as well as the quality of your trust decisions. In addition to your experiences, your willingness to make the effort to get to know others who are "different" from the way you are brings on a 'giant' step in your quest to grow and develop in your understanding of trust, and your growth in the quality of trust that you engage in.

A final addition to this discussion on intrapersonal trust is a discussion on the many tools that exist in assisting one to "know thyself." There are many personality instruments that can give you objective feedback in how you see the world. These are self-assessment questionnaires that are designed to give you information on how you see yourself and advice on how to develop yourself further. These tools include the Myers-Briggs Type Inventory designed by a mother-daughter team and used the world over and translated into more than 25 different languages. This tool has been tested as reliable and valid and is constantly being updated with new research to keep it current. Many people have stated that is has helped them tremendously in understanding themselves and in understanding their family, friends and coworkers. Other tools include the DISC personality inventory, the Enneagram, the Birkman Inventory and many others. If you're willing to be open-minded enough to explore what these self-assessment tools can show you about the way you perceive the world, you may get a head start on understanding how you trust. Regardless of how many times you are disillusioned after placing trust in others, you will believe and have enough confidence in yourself to keep on keeping on, and to keep on trusting.

CHAPTER FOUR

UNDERSTANDING TRUST IN FAMILIES

"Oh, the comfort, the inexpressible comfort of feeling safe with a person, having neither to weigh thoughts…but pouring them all out, just as they are chaff and grain together, certain that a faithful hand will take and sift them, keep what is worth keeping and with a breath of kindness, blow the rest away."
-Anonymous Shoshone Tribal Member

"There is no doubt that it is around the family and
the home that all the
greatest virtues, the most dominating virtues of human society,
are created, strengthened and maintained"
-Winston Churchill

We move from trust in ourselves to understanding trust in families. We know that the family offers a unique perspective and experience concerning trust. Our family of origin imprints on us our very first introduction to life. We are essentially a blank slate when we enter the world. We obviously have no predisposition toward any values or way of thinking and feeling about the world around us. Though we do have our individual personalities, our understanding of the environment we live in and our initial behavior is shaped by the life circumstances we find in our families. During recent times there has been much discussion and emphasis placed on the functional vs. dysfunctional family. It is not my intent to look at the pathological side of family development, but in attempting to understand the role that trust plays in our family situations, it is inevitable that we will indirectly be exposed to the unfolding of dysfunctional families. So where do we start?

Research indicates that a nurturing childhood produces a trusting adult. But there are as many ways to nurture as there are people in the world. Is it simply insuring that a child is nutritionally and properly fed? Or that a child has warm/cool clothes or the latest trendy clothes? Or perhaps that a child has the best shelter there is to offer with a room of his/her own? While this is a form of nurturing, it is astute to say that the nurturing that engenders trust involves far more meaningful actions. As has been stated before, trusting others is really about trusting ourselves, and trusting ourselves begins with self-acceptance. So now we come to the family. In this situation, how does one gain self-acceptance early in life? Our early interactions with family members are where we begin to see ourselves through other's eyes. As mentioned, we enter this world with a blank slate on which we start registering other people's reactions to ourselves as individuals and as family members. We also begin to register the values that are demonstrated to us by these family members. As infants, how are we held? Played with? How much time is spent with us by parents or guardians or others in the home? What are the reactions to our periods of fussiness? During the first couple of years in our lives, do we get the feeling that who we are is OK? That how we express ourselves or think or talk are also OK? Of course gentle admonitions are equally important if children are intruding on someone else's rights or being disrespectful in any way. As a child, when you spoke or offered some information, did you feel honored and respected? Why all these questions? Because your first introduction to others' reactions to you, as well as your reaction to your own environment plays a major role in your decision (and it is a decision) to trust. This is what is meant by being raised in a nurturing environment, one in which an individual is made to feel accepted, respected and honored for who s/he is. This is indeed the first step in moving toward a trusting relationship with a family and with the world around you.

In addition to childhood treatment, another area that greatly affects trust in families is that of values. What morals does a family adopt and adhere to, and how do these chosen values affect the family members? As with our initial look at the concept of trust (second chapter), and afterward a personal look at trust (third chapter), let us attempt to understand how trust operates in families by examining how the descriptors of trust express themselves in family relationships.

HONESTY

Our first descriptor is that of honesty. Without question, honesty plays the largest role in functional vs. dysfunctional families. To the degree that honesty is practiced and maintained determines the psychological healthiness of a particular family environment. So what does honesty look like in a family? First, we have parents or a single parent or guardian, not only being clear about what family rules, expectations, behaviors and values are within the family circle, but most importantly insuring that these rules, expectations and values are properly role-modeled so that children gain a clear understanding of what is expected…what these things "look like." So often we find that parents say one thing and do another, a sort of "do as I say but not as I do" attitude. Not only does this confuse the child, but it gives rise to feelings of doubt, confusion, anger and possibly depression..

In addition to clarity and positive role modeling, honesty expresses itself in demonstrating to siblings that not only do they have different personalities, talents and gifts, but that all these differences are valued equally; in other words, one sibling is not favored over another because of these differences. It is true that it is easier to relate to some personalities than others, including one's own children's personalities, especially when their preferences in values and habits in life are the same as the parents. It's more trying to deal with children whose personalities, preferences and likes and dislikes are quite different from those of the parents. To maintain honesty in the family it is so important that every member of a family is made to feel valued, loved, honored and respected for who they are.

What about the concepts of lying, cheating and keeping secrets? We have briefly addressed these concepts in the first few chapters but let's take a look at how these concepts are expressed in family life. Lying, of course, is unacceptable behavior, as it sets a negative tone in the family's daily activities, and also because the person who is lied to or lied about feels betrayed, rejected and humiliated. As child psychologists tell us, young children (primarily ages 4-5) often make up stories and tell tall tales. This may be considered normal activity at this age because children enjoy hearing stories and making up stories for fun. These young children may blur the distinction between reality and fantasy. However, older children and adolescents who now know the difference between made-up stories and reality may lie to be self-serving in some way. If this behavior is not addressed, they acquire a sense of "getting away with it." And like any other habit, once an action is tried and meets with success, the temptation to continue lying grows stronger. If the parent, parents or guardian address the situation immediately, there will be a reason, support and understanding for the child to engage in honesty in all aspects of life. The lesson is that one lie leads to another and another until eventually it is embedded in the subconscious. Sooner or later the "liar" will discover that lies can unravel and expose the liar. Once a person has gained a reputation as a liar, they find that they are not trusted by others. And it becomes a monumental task to overcome that reputation. As stated before, trust is very fragile, and once broken it is a hard long road back to regaining the trust that once was given freely. While we stated that this book is not about pathological or dysfunctional families, it is true that if a family member is an alcoholic, drug or otherwise addicted individual, the lies necessary to cover up that addiction can irreparably damage the family's trust level. Even if the addict recovers, the residual feelings of anger and betrayal will always exist.

What about cheating and stealing? Basically, cheating and stealing are about taking something which doesn't belong to you, or misrepresenting certain facts. These actions can be expressed in different ways – for instance, cheating on an exam at school by passing off someone else's work as your own. This action has serious consequences for the cheater: there's the fear of getting caught, the knowledge of knowing yourself as a fraud, the repercussions of being found out, etc. But the worst form of cheating as expressed in families, is when marriage partners violate their vows to each other. This form of cheating affects each and every family member in varying degrees and has long-lasting effects. Yes, there are extenuating circumstances, but the results are the same – family members range from being disturbed to being fearful to being resentful (resentment being defined as a hardened form of anger.) In the case of broken families, the child who has to switch from one family to another and possibly to yet another will most likely have trust issues for perhaps a lifetime.

As regards stealing, when family members do not respect each other's property or the property of others outside of their family circles, an essential part of trust is lost, and that is respect for others. If the child's own property is not respected, the repercussions can range from anger to depression. If children observe their parents or guardian taking materials and supplies from the workplace to the home – regardless of how the parents admonish the children that stealing is unacceptable behavior, they will translate the parents' actions as an "OK" thing to do despite what they say. This of course can easily lead to the children taking things that are important to them, such as electronic equipment and clothes from stores, as well as taking the property of classmates. In our geographical area in the past year, two children have lost their lives over a stolen jacket and a stolen bike...this is the extreme price to pay for not teaching and enforcing the need to respect others and their property.

You may wish to post your reflections or comments on www. trustontrial.com

Question: How was honesty demonstrated in your family during your formative years?

Reflections: Did you try lying and stealing during your younger years? Were you found out? How did your parents or guardians deal with any dishonesty that you may have displayed?

COMMITMENT

Another trust descriptor that we have addressed is commitment. In looking at trust in a general sense we described commitment as a sense of "ya gotta wanna." We've also stated that commitment is about taking responsibility and accountability for whatever pledge or promise you have made. In a family situation, commitment is a dedication to maintaining and preserving a cohesive, productive and healthy family group. Commitment is all about a decision – a decision to be faithful to family members and family values, and assist in family difficulties. This faithfulness generally expresses itself as being supportive in times of need. It can be devastating to one family member to look for support from the other family members during a difficult time only to discover that the family members are too busy in their own worlds and unwilling to assist. An extreme case of this situation occurs when a family member commits suicide and others in the family realize that the depression signs were there but they just didn't notice. This situation, of course, has harmful results that can last a lifetime.

You may wish to post your reflections or comments on www.trustontrial.com

Question: How was commitment demonstrated in your family during your formative years?

Reflections: Did your parents commit themselves to your healthy growth and development? Did you feel you were a valued member of the family?

SINCERITY

The trust descriptor of sincerity is particularly meaningful in a family situation. We have described this descriptor as being embodied in the saying "say what you mean and mean what you say." And again, this descriptor needs primarily to be demonstrated and role-modeled by the parent, parents or guardians. Have you ever heard a child say to its parent, "Yeah, Mom (or Dad), that's what you always say" implying that the parent says one thing but doesn't always follow through. To a child it can be very disappointing when a parent says or promises something and isn't true to his or her word. Parents need to realize that promises should not be made unless they can be truly delivered. A particularly difficult action for children to deal with is that of indifference. When a child asks a question of a parent or guardian and they reply "oh, sure" without giving it any thought, and this action is repeated several times, the child will come to understand (even though they may not be able to express it as such), that the parent or guardian is insincere. Children need to be genuinely listened to, particularly when they are consulting the parents on a matter that is important to them. In this way, they can come to be a valued member of the family. On the other hand, the child itself needs to come to realize through the role modeling of the parents, that they need to mean what they say when it is said. This is the sincerity part of trust – meaning what you say. This sincerity is true not only with family members but with their friends and classmates as well. Through practicing and becoming sincere in our lives, we are learning to be true to ourselves. What emotions are felt by a family member when he or she detects insincerity or lack of genuineness? The minor emotions are annoyance and aggravation – but the major effects are betrayal, anger and a lack of respect for those who prove to be insincere.

You may wish to post your reflections or comments on www. trustontrial.com

Question: How was sincerity demonstrated in your family during your formative years?

Reflections: Did you feel listened to or heard in interactions with family members? Were important promises made in your childhood years, kept by your parents/ guardians?

DEPENDABILITY/RELIABILITY

Let's move on to the trust factors of dependability and reliability. This may seem like an extension of sincerity and commitment, and yes, of course, in some ways it is. It is actually another version of sincerity: instead of the maxim "say what you mean and mean what you say," dependability rather infers "do what you say you're going to do." And as stated previously, since trust is built up over time, we can show that when we do what we say we are going to do, we prove ourselves to be dependable. It can also be said that when we prove ourselves to be unreliable, we are additionally proving that we are uncooperative as well as not being trustworthy. Since our family members are the first individuals in our lives with whom we interact, if our initial exposure proves that we can't depend on others for the most part, then we may learn to depend on ourselves entirely. But there will be many situations in our lives where we will have to depend on others and if the trust level is not there, it will either cause great difficulties for us or it will lead to an unfavorable consequence in the particular situation. In a family situation, if members come to the point where they feel they can't expect reliability or dependability from a certain member, human nature being what it is, they in turn will not extend their reliability and dependability to that family member, resulting in an ineffective family environment.

You may wish to post your reflections or comments on www. trustontrial.com

Question: How was dependability/reliability demonstrated in your family during your formative years?

Reflections: Did you feel you could depend/rely on your family members during your formative years? Did you rely mostly on yourself, or did you feel family members were there for you when you needed them?

LOYALTY

Loyalty is a trust descriptor that we alluded to when we discussed commitment. Loyalty is closely related to commitment, and is thought of as the willingness to be committed through both good and bad times. Does loyalty imply the willingness to persist even in unhealthy and unacceptable situations? We look at the unswerving loyalty of cult members whose community engages in what could be perceived as immoral and unlawful actions. And so we do question their sense of loyalty, as well we should. Is loyalty good or bad? In the questionnaire that was distributed for purposes of research people were asked what words defined trust and many responded with the word "loyalty". We may ask ourselves, what were they thinking? What did they mean when they responded in this manner? From a healthy perspective, loyalty is generally seen as going the distance in a socially acceptable endeavor, and not folding in the towel when life and circumstances begin to get rough. As with the postman who delivers the mail through snow, sleet, mud and all weather elements, loyalty implies we just keep on keeping on with the person or situation to which we have given our loyalty. So how does loyalty express itself in families? As the expression states, "blood is thicker than water," there is a certain bonding and a closeness that can only exist between family members. Of course, we have all seen instances where this bonding does not occur for various reasons. Sometimes an argument occurs between family members who then separate and do not speak with each other for years. Obviously, this is a dysfunctional way to handle differences that can occur frequently among family members. How do parents or guardians instill a sense of loyalty that engenders trust and does not become destructive? Again, the main rule is to demonstrate and role-model the loyalty behavior that would encourage children to emulate this behavior. What does this role modeling behavior look like? Perhaps the best practice to engage in is to ensure that no one in the family ever speaks negatively or against another family member. If someone has a complaint against another family member, the best way to deal with this complaint is to address that family member personally and privately with respect. In role modeling loyal behavior, parents need never complain or deride either the marriage partner or the children in front of other family members. Being able to accomplish this suggests a demonstration of the highest form of loyalty in a family situation. When every family member can say that, despite the family difficulties that occur on a daily basis, they still feel loved and wanted, then you indeed have a family that is practicing love and loyalty.

You may wish to post your reflections or comments on www. trustontrial.com

Question: How was loyalty demonstrated in your family during your formative years?

Reflections: Did your siblings support each other in front of non-family members? Other than "name calling" and sibling rivalry, did family members "stick up" for each other in front of non-family members?

FAIRNESS

In the family context, fairness is often seen as not favoring one family member over another. However, children often feel that unless everyone is treated the same exact way, then parents are being unfair. As we have stated, treating each child the same way may not be the fair thing to do, as children are different in their needs, wants and desires. Explaining this fact to children is difficult since they simply feel they are not getting what they want. It is difficult, but it would behoove parents to continuously check as to whether they may be favoring one child over another because of gender, behavioral characteristics, abilities, tendencies, and talents. And of course, there are situations when fairness is obvious to everyone involved, and therefore speaks for itself. In a family of two children, if at Christmastime, one child receives a significantly greater number of presents than the other child consistently through the years, fairness definitely comes into question. In being fair in families, the main rule of thumb is that fairness is measured by the acceptance that each child feels in the family forum.

You may wish to post your reflections or comments on www. trustontrial.com

<u>Question:</u>   How was fairness demonstrated in your family during your formative years?

<u>Reflections:</u>   Did you feel you were treated "fairly" as a child by your parents and family members? Why or why not? How has this affected your sense of fairness?

FAITH/CONFIDENCE

Belief, as we have stated, is defined as a confidence in the truth or existence of something not immediately susceptible to rigorous proof. If children believe their parents, guardians or teachers are heroes, they do so with a solid, unshakable belief. Belief has something in common with fairness in that actions are seen and interpreted through the eyes of the beholders. Beliefs are some of the strongest motivators to be found in our society, and of course they are developed at home. It's possible that many people hold their beliefs in the form of religion, but a sense of belief or faith is expressed in many other ways than religion. As we hear and view the wartime atrocities occurring in our world even as we speak, we wonder how to reconcile a doctrine of love, forgiveness and acceptance of others with the torturing, maiming and killing of people of different races and creeds. If this is difficult for adults to understand, then how much more the difficulty when children are involved? Research has been conducted with children who have grown up from infancy knowing only war and hate. One obviously does not have to be told that these children, for the most part, have a most convoluted idea of the concept of trust.

In the family, the most powerful thing parents can do for their children is to teach them to believe in themselves. Teaching children that they are indeed capable, competent, talented and lovable individuals who can accomplish whatever they commit themselves to with perseverance and dedication, is a productive way for them to learn the characteristics of faith and confidence. This belief in themselves can be bolstered through acknowledging, upholding, respecting, honoring and accepting the child for who she or he is. Also important is emphasizing to children that others they deal with are also capable, competent, talented and lovable individuals deserving of respect and honor.

You may wish to post your reflections or comments on www. trustontrial.com

Question: How was faith and confidence demonstrated in your family during your formative years?

Reflections: What role did faith and confidence play in your family environment? Did you feel confident in your role as a family member? Why or why not?

In concluding our discussion of understanding trust in families, we remind ourselves that families are the first introduction for infants to explore and interpret how the world operates and determine how much individuals in this world can be trusted. It is with our family that we discover who we are and what kind of world we live in.

"Call it a clan, call it a network, call it a tribe, call it a family.
Whatever
you call it, whoever you are, you need one."
-Jane Howard Neville
Countess of Westmoreland (1533-1593)

CHAPTER FIVE

EXAMINING TRUST IN ORGANIZATIONS

> "If we can by any method establish
> a relation of mutual trust between
> the laborer and the employer, we shall lay
> the foundation stone of a
> structure that will endure for all time."
> *-Mark Hanna*
> *American Industrialist (1837-1904)*

With all the rapid changes that are occurring in society, one of the areas most greatly affected is business – organizations and companies. Many of these changes have affected the very core of the way business is conducted. What has contributed to these changes? Two major reasons attributed to these changes are the onset of worldwide competition and the tremendous impact technology is having in every aspect of doing business. Beginning in the 1980's, with the advent of mergers, acquisitions, reorganizations, leveraged buyouts, layoffs and downsizings, and other 'innovative' business practices, the work environment has been tossed about. These business practices led to the downfall of the old psychological work contract which was primarily characterized by loyalty, commitment and longevity. A general definition of a psychological work contract includes mutual expectations between employers and employees. It was defined as 'psychological' because it wasn't spoken but implied. Under the old psychological work contract, employees dedicated themselves to the mission and vision of the organization and the organization rewarded them with benefits and lifetime employment. The expectation was that if you worked hard and dedicated yourself and didn't violate any of the policies, then work as usual would continue. The new work contract is different. While both parties still mutually agree that, as before, commitment to the organization's policies is expected, now the relationship is finite and exists only as it benefits the employer. If the employer determines that they are not making enough profit, they will counteract this expectation basically through downsizing the employee workforce or outsourcing some of its functions to countries with a cheaper labor force. Employees can no longer have the expectation that if they dedicate themselves to the company, their jobs will remain. The new psychological work contract has evolved into a situation where lifetime employment is gone. It's become clear that the company for which an employee is now working could vanish or be reshaped with no job guarantee for anyone. In addition, the workforce is expected to do more with fewer resources. This means that as companies reorganize and jobs are eliminated, these employees are not replaced, and those who remain after the downsizing are required to pick up the slack left by those employees who are no longer there. Since additional resources, more often than not, are not allocated to cover the loss of extra hands, those remaining employees carry a double load. Much has been written about the 'survivor syndrome' which alludes to the guilt that the remaining employees experience because their coworkers were eliminated and they remained. Also adding to this pressure is the extra workload these employees must carry. These same employees are also wondering when the other shoe will fall and they themselves will lose their jobs.

Profits now no longer suggest a healthy margin but rather are identified in terms of exponentially increasing margins. The new values are more closely aligned with greed, which is defined in the workplace as the need for an excessive amount of profit. This new value was first heard in the movie (movies have always been regarded as a medium which accurately reflects a society's changing values), "Wall Street" when the actor Michael Douglas utters the words "greed is good." This new margin of profit was to benefit only the executives and owners and was not extended down the line to the actual workers. This new value allowed CEOs and their executive counterparts to shower themselves with luxuries and take from the coffers what was never intended for their personal use. Boards of Directors across the country were and are voting in excessive pay salaries and benefits to these executives on the stated reason that it's necessary to provide these outlandish salaries to get experienced talent. As company after company goes bankrupt, this reasoning has since been proven false and invalid in every aspect. These practices, which in some cases are still in place, have led to ever increasing downsizings and layoffs as we now find ourselves in the midst of a severe major economic downturn.

SEVERAL GENERATIONS IN THE WORKFORCE

Another dramatic change exists in today's present workforce: The number of identified generations in the workforce is higher than it has ever been in the history of our country. A generation can be defined as a group of individuals, most of whom are the same approximate age, having similar ideas, problems, attitudes, etc. For many years, a generation was defined by its values and signature events, and occurred no more that every 10+ years. Because of the rapid changes in today's society, the number of years defining a generation has been decreasing. Researchers tell us that defining values and signature events (WWII, the Civil Rights explosion of the 60's, Vietnam War, the Challenger explosion, the fall of the Berlin Wall, the terrorist attack of 9/11/2001, etc.) are affecting our youth every 3 to 5 years, resulting in generations being formed much more rapidly. We note that there are some generations in today's workforce who have never experienced lifelong employment and have known only downsizings, restructurings, mergers, acquisitions and so forth.

Still present in today's workforce (and because of the economic situation in our country, are likely to retain a presence even longer), is what is commonly referred to as the Traditionalist generation. This is the generation that Tom Brokaw referred to in his book as "The Greatest Generation." The signature events for this generation include the Depression of the 30's and the major war of the 40's. One of the characteristics defining this generation is loyalty – one of our identified trust factors. This generation strongly feels that once you establish a long-term relationship with an individual or organization, you remain true to that relationship. They are not considered a "fair weather" generation, but are in the relationship for the long haul. This generation was particularly affected by the downsizings that began en masse in the 1980's. Along with the Baby Boomers, they had fought for their work rights with employers through their unions, particularly in the 40's through the 60's and were settled into the psychological work contract which we have discussed existed then. These downsizings were considered a striking blow to their value system and to their understanding of loyalty, and they felt violated by this new workforce strategy. Other generations were obviously affected by this massive change but not as strongly as the Traditionalists. This generation also had the strongest work ethic, hard work being expected and understood. It was understood that this generation was identified as being the most challenged by technology, which we have noted has had a tremendous effect on today's work environment. However, this identification is being diluted as older workers take to their computers more frequently and efficiently.

The next identified generation is the "Baby Boomers." The official dates for this generation are 1946 through 1964 (United States Census Bureau), with some researchers indicating that there were actually different phases within this generation. This by far is the largest generation, covering a span of almost 20 years, and the sheer size of it greatly impacted society. The predominant characteristics and value system of this generation included: embracing change, fighting for a cause and social justice, and engaging in competition in order to achieve success. At work this generation also has a strong work ethic in reference to pursuing promotions and prestige.

Generation X is comprised of those individuals born between 1964 and 1980. This is the generation that had seen their parents, relatives, neighbors and others experience the downsizings, layoffs, etc. begun in the 1980's, and felt their devastation and wounded pride as they were 'let go' and sometimes referred to as 'superfluous personnel.' Around this same time technology was 'catching on' and they were the generation that did the 'catching on.' They understood, studied and reveled in the potential of this technology. However, they had no intention of allowing their newfound knowledge and skills to be usurped by corporate America and being 'dumped' by these same organizations when they became "superfluous". Bill Gates and Steve Jobs are members of this generation, and represent the entrepreneurial spirit which greatly characterizes it. With this generation, loyalty became a value of the past, to be superseded by independence and creativity.

Generation Y, also known as the Milennials, are those born between 1977 and 1994. They make up over 20% of today's generations. The parents of this generation were very involved in their children's development; consequently, their parents are still very involved in their coming of age. Examples abound of the parents' 'extreme' influence in their children's lives; for instance, a story was reported on the internet of an incident where a mother called her son's boss and asked why he had treated her son in a certain way. These parents are sometimes referred to as "helicopter parents." This term is a colloquial, early 21st-century term used particularly at educational institutions for a parent who pays extremely close attention to his or her child's experiences and problems. They are so named because, like helicopters, they hover closely overhead, rarely out of reach, whether their children need them or not. This action was unheard of in previous generations. It is estimated this generation will have impressed their brand of change on the workplace after we have weathered the extremely poor economic conditions that we are experiencing today in business.

Given the description of today's work environment, we begin examining the trust factors in business and how they apply to today's workplace.

HONESTY

"The glue that holds all relationships together --
including the relationship
between the leader and the led --
is trust, and trust is based on integrity."

-Brian Tracy
Chairman, Brian Tracy International (1944-   )

As in other areas of our lives, honesty plays the largest role in affecting our ability to trust. So what does honestly look like in the workplace? We can start with how an organization describes itself to the rest of the world, and these descriptions can be found in the organization's stated mission, vision and values. These stated values can be found in their annual reports, and some companies clearly distribute their mission, vision and values to their employees. These values also describe the organizational culture, which is defined as the shared beliefs and values that influence the behavior of all the organizational members, or the intentionally created work environment within which employees operate. So what values has your organization adopted? How does it say it represents itself to the nation? If you were to peruse the vision and values statements of several companies, you would find that most of them refer to honesty and integrity as their standard for conducting business. The big question of course always is: how are these values actually practiced in daily operations?

In the "Organizational Behavior" classes that I have taught at several universities, there have been many personal stories told by distraught employees who have been required by their employers to engage in knowingly unlawful and illegal acts. These employees were forced to face their own consciences in either complying with these requests or making the difficult decision to leave the company. Given today's poor economic conditions, this would entail joining the hordes of job seekers looking for employment…a very tough decision to make. Are these companies adhering to their stated values to be honest in all of their dealings? Stories also related by students are those that involve their putting their heart, soul and hard work into a particular project only to have their supervisors or other company officials take credit for the work that they produced without any recognition or acknowledgement of their roles. This action is known as plagiarism in the workplace. Executives in these companies seem to not be aware that these acts of dishonesty cause not only distrust but anger in their employees. However, there are times when the employees themselves don't live up to the organizational stated values. The other side of the story is when managers and supervisors take their coaching and mentoring roles seriously and reach out to the employees only to find themselves maligned by these same employees. These differences in employee behavior can be directly attributed to the generational differences that we have just discussed. Different generations have different value systems and express them in the workplace. As with being a parent, coach, teacher or any other position in which influence over others is exerted, one influences either negatively or positively – very seldom is an authority's influence felt in a neutral manner. It sometimes seems like a no-win situation…it is very difficult. However, there is a simple but effective rule that can almost always eventually lead to good results and that is – when the supervisor or manager 'role models' the behavior that they in turn expect from the employees, they are much more likely to meet with success and engender trust in the workplace. This may be a time consuming process but almost always yields positive results. Consequently, this implies that the values an organization espouses must indeed be found within the individuals who manage the organization. If honesty is a value that an organization declares is true of their culture, then honesty must be found within the value systems of all those managers and executives who implement rules and regulations and manage that culture. Obviously, this implies that those individuals found in the highest levels of the organization need to be role modeling those values – especially honesty – to its managers and supervisors. We all recognize that the leaders set the tone for the organizational culture. If there continues to be discrepancies between what the leaders say are the organizational values and what is role modeled in the behavior of these leaders then we understand that this dishonesty creates distrust. After repeated incidences of dishonesty in the workplace, the morale will be affected and productivity will decrease.

Another issue that affects trust is violence and change in the workplace. As always in cases of human behavior, the greater the stress and pressure employees experience in the workplace, the greater the possibility of 'explosions' resulting from this poor work environment (much like a volcano operates as pressure builds up from within). Violence in the workplace has increased significantly in this last decade and research would tell us that a negative work environment can contribute significantly to that violence. Are we saying that a negative workplace environment is the sole contributor to this violence? No, of course not, but it is a contributor. Another major contributor to workplace violence is the increasing rapidity of change that we have been addressing, and the instability and chaos that results from this change. Because of their background experiences and value systems, some employees are better able than others to cope with changes. When organizations carefully select and declare what their values are and consequently select and hire workers whose values most resemble the organization's stated values, true and productive success can result. In my ongoing experience as a Career Transition Consultant, I advise former employees who have been laid off as a result of downsizing to seek positions in companies that appear to practice their stated values and focus their efforts on working for those companies. Again, a dose of reality tells us that all things do change, and in both our personal and work lives, circumstances do change which may in turn change our value systems. It becomes imperative that we keep up with these changes in both our personal and work lives.

You may wish to post your reflections or comments on www. trustontrial.com

Question: What has been your experience with honesty in organizations?

Reflections: Do you find it difficult to be honest in the workplace? Have you worked for an organization that practices its value of honesty?

SINCERITY

"To give real service you must add something which cannot be bought or measured with money, and that is sincerity and integrity."

-Douglas Adams
British writer, dramatist and musician (1952-2001)

We have stated that our motto, if you will, for sincerity is "say what you mean and mean what you say." As we discussed, insincerity is the greatest deterrent after honesty to building trust as it gives rise to feelings of abandonment, rejection and eventually anger. How would insincerity be expressed in organizations? An example would be the motivational programs that are introduced into the workplace to encourage and develop productivity. As these types of programs continue to be introduced into the workplace, employees tend to refer to them as the "flavor of the month" programs. These programs can in fact be very effective in and of themselves; however, how they are introduced and managed will steer the course of their success or failure. For instance, after a particular program is introduced, some employees may become very enthused and put their hearts and souls into applying the concepts and implementing the program with the understanding that they will be acknowledge and perhaps rewarded for their efforts. But they come to realize that their managers are insincere in the sense that the intent was only to make the effort "look good" but not to actually allow any changes to be implemented as a result of the program. Those employees who demonstrated sincerity in their efforts become disillusioned and consequently cynical when the next "flavor of the month" program is introduced. It is important to note that at times managers are overwhelmed by the amount of programs they are expected to introduce and manage and as a defense against time constraints, they become insincere in their efforts to see these programs through. A more honest effort would involve introducing fewer programs and devoting time, attention and reward systems for those employees who apply themselves to these programs and distinguish themselves in their productivity.

You may wish to post your reflections or comments on www. trustontrial.com

Question: What has been your experience with sincerity in the workplace?

<u>Reflections</u>:   How can an organization best express its sincerity to its employees? How is sincerity built or destroyed in the workplace?

COMMITMENT

"Unless commitment is made, there are only promises and hopes; but no plans."

-Peter F. Drucker
American Management Consultant, Author (1909-2005)

Commitment, as stated before, is represented by the saying "ya gotta wanna." No one can force another to be committed to a work project. This is entirely an intrinsic motivation as it comes from within. It is demonstrated in the form of enthusiasm and a "stick-to-itivity" attitude. Employees see the project or process through regardless of obstacles, barriers and tribulations. How does an organization encourage commitment from its employees? We have already mentioned the need to role model the behavior that is expected from others. When a manager assigns employees to a project for any length of time, then the expectation is that the company will allocate the necessary resources and support that the project may require. This action demonstrates commitment to the project and to the employees. A frequent complaint from employees is the rejection that they experience when an organization for no apparent reason starts pulling out resources and support from a particular project without a sound explanation. This will go a long way in creating distrust with employees and consequently when another project is introduced they will, out of self-defense, reserve their commitment to see, as they say, "which way the wind is blowing." Their initial enthusiasm has now turned to cautiousness and suspicion. Employees have the responsibility as well to take notice when their enthusiasm for a particular project is dying and analyze why. Once the understanding for the dying enthusiasm has been gained then it remains the responsibility of the employee to take corrective action to either recommit or be honest with oneself and withdraw from the project.

You may wish to post your reflections or comments on www. trustontrial.com

Question: What has been your experience with commitment in the workplace?

Reflection: What are the differences between working for an organization that is committed to its employees as opposed to one that is not?

DEPENDABILITY/RELIABILITY

Commitment in turn leads to another trust descriptor in the form of dependability/ reliability. This trust factor is embodied in the statement "do what you say you're going to do." All of us, at one time or another have been victims of feelings of betrayal and anger when a promise was made but never delivered. In the workplace, this lack of dependability and reliability is especially felt when groups of people must work with each other to either create or deliver a product or service. Nothing is more deflating to work enthusiasm and momentum than when a certain group or individual constantly misses deadlines for various reasons. In another sense, the trust factor of dependability is violated when a work group consistently misses its deadlines and is therefore perceived as undependable. When one shows oneself as unreliable then a veil of suspicion is raised by coworkers which may be difficult to remove. This suspicion of unreliability is also seen in the lack of cooperation from certain members of the team. In examining an example of a team of engineers in a manufacturing plant, we find members assigned specific duties within the team in accordance with their talents, capabilities and competencies. As the scenario develops, it becomes clear that certain team members are not sharing information with others, essentially 'guarding' their part of the project. These actions create havoc and result in missed deadlines and the creation of anger and distrust in the workplace. The scenario can be changed to a positive result as the angry team members address the situation with the reluctant and undependable members, and progress and production can be restored. Lack of cooperation goes a long way in destroying team trust and effectiveness and needs to be addressed immediately. Unfortunately, at times irreparable damage can result, and trust is never restored. Lack of dependability from others can take a tremendous toll on the psyche in all areas of one's work life.

You may wish to post your reflections or comments on www. trustontrial.com

Question: What has been your experience with dependability/ reliability in the workplace?

Reflection: Have you had any experience in working with unreliable coworkers? How was this experienced resolved, if at all?

LOYALTY

"The greater the loyalty of a group toward the group, the greater
is the motivation among the members to achieve the goals of the
group, and the greater the probability that the group will achieve its
goals."

-Rensis Likert
American Educator (1903-1981)

Loyalty is another identified trust descriptor and as with fairness, it also "depends" on the intrinsic values of the person describing loyalty. Loyalty is seen as faithfulness to commitments, obligations, people and institutions. As mentioned, the expression of "fair weather fans" in regards to sports teams brings to mind what loyalty doesn't look like, which is being faithful only when life is going well. Conversely, loyalty implies sticking with a person or situation through thick and thin. As we have described the downsizing situations evidenced in today's workforce, it is safe to say that loyalty has been all but destroyed – there essentially is no loyalty in today's organizations. After the record number of downsizings and layoffs in today's work environment, the new work contract is shaping up from the employer's perspective as that of hiring workers as the need dictates, but offloading these same workers when the bottom line doesn't look good. And the younger generations in the workforce who have experienced nothing but downsizings since their tenure in the workplace, have declared that they will work for a company as long as they feel they are being treating well, but will jump ship for greener pastures without a second thought. Today's psychological work contract is still in the process of being unfolded and when it is set, it will look nothing like the previous one of loyalty and commitment. The new psychological work contract could potentially be a sound contract if all the players understand the rules. However, its potential for building trust is not strong at this time.

You may wish to post your reflections or comments on www. trustontrial.com

Question: What has been your experience with loyalty in the workplace?

Reflections: How much loyalty are you willing to give to your employer? How much do you expect from your employer in return?

FAIRNESS

"The value of having everybody get the complete picture and trusting each person with it far outweighs the risk involved."
-Bill Gates
American business magnate, Chairman of Microsoft (1955-   )

The trust factor of fairness is very difficult to assess, as we have already discussed. As mentioned, what may be fair to one person may not be fair to another. This is especially true in the workplace. Motivation in the workplace is primarily addressed by the reward systems an organization has to offer. Fairness in this case is expressed as consistency in applying rewards. If a worker performs a certain activity in a certain way with a certain effectiveness and a reward is applied, then when a similar activity is performed by another worker in a similar way, the expectation is that the same reward will be applied. However, as all managers and employees know, this is not the case for various reasons and not always possible. Consequently, some workers are rewarded and others not for performing similar duties. We are aware that nothing destroys enthusiasm and commitment more than when a person or a group of people perceive that they have been "unfairly" treated. We have experienced incredible legislation from both federal and state governing bodies that has attempted to induce fair and equitable treatment in the workplace. However, as we have discussed, we know that treating all cases and all people equally may not ultimately be the fair thing to do. So what are organizations and managers to do when attempting to be fair? Two avenues can be taken when addressing this issue and they are: 1) be consistent to the degree possible when rewarding employees, and 2) be honest and act with integrity in dealing with all employees. Explaining to people why a certain direction is taken or why a certain decision has been made goes a long way in helping them to understand and accept the direction or decision. It is amazing how many times organizations and institutions make decisions and take actions without a word of explanation to those who are greatly affected by these decisions and actions. Better yet, research has shown that when employees are allowed to participate in the decision-making process to whatever degree possible, the decision will be better implemented by these same employees. Employees are valued for their input and the process of building trust is made stronger.

Again, fairness is a very difficult trust factor to build in an organization but it can be done to most everyone's satisfaction. Fairness in the workplace is demonstrated as a sincere attempt to consider all the particulars of the workforce (i.e. EEO factors and other workforce characteristics) and combine them with the needs and requirements of the organization, and then proceed with decisions and activities that address as many of these concerns as possible.

You may wish to post your reflections or comments on www. trustontrial.com

Question: What has been your experience with fairness in the workplace?

Reflections: Has there been a time in your working experience when you felt that you hadn't been treated fairly by management? What was the outcome?

FAITH/CONFIDENCE

"When we consider a project, we really study it — not just the surface idea, but everything about it. And when we go into that new project, we believe in it all the way. We have confidence in our ability to do it right."

-Walt Disney
Co-Founder of Walt Disney Productions (1901-1966)

As before, the last two trust factors will be addressed together as they imply similar meanings. For instance, having faith or believing in the leader of an organization or one's manager or supervisor also implies having confidence in their knowledge, skills and abilities. There are some leaders and managers who are so charismatic that followers find themselves willing to believe in them merely because of their charisma. However, there are some leaders and managers who have earned our trust because of their role modeling of behaviors that inspire trust such as has been discussed. With faith and confidence we learn to come to trust ourselves and our own intuition. Conversely, when our belief and trust is violated, we begin to question ourselves – our values, our understanding of who we are, our ability to reason effectively.

In applying the trust factors to organizations, we have addressed how the lack of these trust factors can damage the organizational culture, and how including and practicing these factors can lead to more satisfied and productive employees and a successful organization.

You may wish to post your reflections or comments on www. trustontrial.com

Question: What has been your experience with faith/confidence in the workplace?

Reflection: Has your faith in a boss or leader ever been destroyed....how so?

CHALLENGE: We will end the discussion of the trust factors in organizations with a challenge. The Ponemon Institute, an information security research company, and TRUSTe, the most widely recognized privacy trustmark company on the Web conducted a two-stage survey to gauge the privacy policies and practices of leading consumer brands. They engaged 6,500 people -- weighted by age, gender and household income to match the U.S. census -- to name the companies they trusted most with their privacy. The survey was completed and the Most Trusted Companies for Privacy Awards were extended to the winners. In the spirit of encouraging readers to do their own research, I would encourage you to research which companies made it to the Top Ten. Please share your findings, reflections and comments on the website www.trustontrial.com.

CHAPTER SIX

SO WHAT? NOW WHAT?

So finally at the end of all our discussions and attempts to understand trust....we step back to look at it all and ask ourselves – so what? Why all this commotion over trust?

SO WHAT?

In discussing and understanding the concept of trust in our personal, family and organizational lives, we have identified, through research, eight characteristics that must be present, to some degree or another, in order for us to understand and assess how we trust. We now know that without the presence of at least some of these characteristics, we most likely will not end up in successful trusting relationships. As we have stated repeatedly throughout our discussion, we live in interesting times. Given these very interesting times in which we live, the "so what" becomes very important. As we look around us and review the tremendous changes that have occurred in our society and on the planet in the last 10 years, we realize how rapidly life and the world has changed around us.

Change of Values. Just take a look at the tremendous change of values this country has experienced in areas that were once held dear in every aspect of our daily lives. The original values set forth by our founding fathers were reflected in all of the 8 trust factors we have just discussed....honesty, sincerity, consistency, dependability, commitment, loyalty, and faithfulness/confidence. However, as discussed previously in this book, particularly in the chapter on organizations, we see how these values have been changed over time and by different generations to reflect what we are experiencing in our present-day culture. In business, in politics, in education, in religion, in real estate, in finance and ultimately in all walks of our daily lives, we have seen our values change to the degree that, for the most part, they barely reflect the basic core values originally intended by these founding fathers. Yes, of course, after over 200 years, we can come to expect changes in values. But our basic core values need not change significantly. The French have a saying "Plus que ca change, plus que c'est la même chose" which translated means "The more things change, the more they remain the same." Our basic core values might be altered over time and by different generations but need to remain essentially the same in order for society to be stable and productive. If values change significantly and rapidly, it's easy to understand the disorder and chaos that would result. An unknown operating value spreads fear and of course, distrust, which is the 'So What?' of our discussion. It becomes crucial for each of us to understand what values we hold as individuals, as families, as organizational workers and as citizens of our country.

Past Decade. In reviewing the events of the past few years in the United States, readers may be shocked at the innumerable media reports of dishonest acts in all walks of our daily lives. As we discussed in the previous chapter, reports of dishonesty, cheating, stealing, fraud, embezzlement, hypocrisy and other negative behaviors have been reported in all aspects of public life including: business, finance, religion, all forms of government (federal, state and local), politics, real estate, healthcare and academia. From a trust perspective, it's easy to see how the trust level in the leadership of all public areas of this country has been rapidly eroding – almost as quickly as the melting ice in the polar ice caps. The "so what?" question of this chapter brings the strong realization of the tremendous task of rebuilding these major industries when the very trust in the leadership required to do so is at an all-time low. What will trust in leadership look like as we face this rebuilding task? There is no question that this rebuilding effort will require the effort of every American to become involved in a constructive manner in whatever way they can. But as discussed constantly in this book, it will be incumbent on each individual to ensure that s/he examines and understands his/her relationship to the concept of trust, so as to better contribute to the reshaping of America. The public redefinition of trust in leadership will evolve in time as individuals, families and organizations become involved in this reshaping process.

Present Day. A general definition of trust will evolve for this country over a period of time as individuals come to understand what trust means to them and also which definition of trust they will use as their basic operating value. How can one really "trust" someone else if it's unknown what is meant by trust, what the consequences of violated trust will be, and what needs to be done to regain that violated trust? It becomes crucial that we enter future trust relationships at every level with an awareness of the trust process that is occurring and the consequences of violated trust. Again, in times of great change, such as the times we now live in, each individual must decide for himself/herself, what is important to him/her concerning the decision to trust. No longer can any of us afford to sit back, shake our heads and say "ain't it awful?" Nor can we fall back into the mode of allowing others to do our thinking for us. While folks around us are more than happy to tell us their viewpoints, their perspectives, their perceptions, their understandings, their wants, their needs, their desires, their decisions, and all their other leanings, in the end each individual needs to think it through and come up with his/her own understandings. And should there be a violation of trust, again we'll hear about other people's reactions, their answers, their feelings, their opinions, their reflections, their interpretations, and their conclusions. But what really matters is the research and the conclusions that individuals have come up with for themselves. Should we not listen to what others have to say? Yes, of course, we respectfully listen to them, especially if they are in turn listening to our perspectives. The problematic situation is one where we listen to others but they negate, disaffirm or disallow our opinions and perspectives. This may tend to erode our healthy self-esteem. However, as we will discuss, the willingness to listen to others is a critical aspect of critical thinking skills that must be developed in order for individuals to form a solid basis on which to come to a clear understanding and definition of trust. We have now arrived at the NOW WHAT? question.

NOW WHAT?

After all this discussion on trust, its definition, its application, its implications, and its impact on our lives, now what do we do with all this knowledge we've gained? What are some of the key actions that will assist us in making good "trust" decisions in our lives? In our Introduction, we stated that there are three applications that can positively shape the trust decisions we make. They are: 1) the Triple A Approach, 2) the necessity for employing effective critical thinking skills, and 3) the need for understanding and utilizing emotional intelligence and the role it plays in our decisions. In the introduction, we made a brief reference to these three approaches; now we will revisit them to discuss them at length.

TRIPLE "A" APPROACH

As mentioned, this concept evolved over the many years I taught courses in colleges and universities. Regardless of what subject you are preparing to study or what skill you are looking to develop, the need for taking in information in an orderly and sequential manner is essential to learning and can be obtained through this approach. We first encountered the Triple A approach in the Introduction to this book. In review, AAA stands for: A=aware, A=alert and A=action.

First "A" – Awareness

The importance of this first "A" becomes apparent in understanding that generally we are not aware of situations and circumstances that surround us. We find ourselves distracted with our daily lives and tend to not pay attention to what is happening around us. We live in an Information Age where we have access to much more information than we can ever hope to fully gain awareness of and comprehend. As a defense mechanism, our reaction is to remain oblivious to much of the information around us to prevent our becoming overwhelmed. However, concentrating on those situations and circumstances that have the greatest impact on us is one of the best places to start in our desire to be "aware" of our immediate world. A definition of "aware" would include descriptors like having knowledge, being conscious and being informed of situations and surroundings. Being aware is most important in preventing accidents, disappointments, tragedies, calamities, misery, and harm in our lives. Obviously, the best way to "have knowledge, be conscious and informed" is to educate yourself regarding your situations and surroundings. We can agree that the way to educate yourself and gain knowledge can range from reading journals, books, and newspapers; to browsing the internet; to listening to educational television programs, our friends, members of our churches; to conducting research and taking how-to classes and courses for degree programs; and finally, to sharing and discussing information with friends and families. By gathering in this information, individuals become aware of what's happening in the world around them and come to understand the implications of the information they are taking in. In reading, listening, and sharing with others, we are not only learning but are also developing and refining this awareness.

So why emphasize awareness in a discussion of trust? As we study and become aware of the behavior patterns of those near to us, we detect various personality patterns and value systems. It is generally accepted that we tend to trust those who are like us – those who share our history, our nationality, our religion, our belief systems, our customs, and especially our value systems. Conversely, we tend to distrust those who are not like us. In our country, we have spent the last two centuries recognizing, understanding and instituting laws compelling us to accept these differences so that we do not discriminate against any of these "differences." It is clear that though we have made great strides in this direction, we still have a way to go. As we have already stated, fear is the prime motivator in generating distrust of others who are "different" from the way we are. We are talking about the fear of the unknown. The best way to overcome this fear of the unknown is to educate ourselves about those who we may neither be fully aware nor understand. In doing so, we begin to connect. This connection goes a long way in our ultimate decision to trust or not to trust. We then apply our knowledge to people's actions and notice their tendencies to be honest, sincere, committed, consistent, reliable, faithful, loyal and confident. As we can see, gathering knowledge and awareness is an important first step to take in a decision to trust.

Second "A" – Alertness

Once individuals have disciplined themselves to become more aware of whom they are and of the world around them, they are much more apt to "notice" when a pattern develops, a repetition occurs, or something out of the ordinary presents itself. In becoming alert, individuals become more observant and circumspect, that is, more watchful, vigilant and guarded. Alertness to patterns and the distinctive combinations of qualities, characteristics and tendencies found in the personalities of those we deal with on a daily basis better prepares us to deal with situations in a more forthright manner. In being observant of these patterns, characteristics and qualities, we can become effective at predicting or foreseeing how an individual might act. The same is true of situations, circumstances and events. For the most part, we become accustomed to these patterns until something occurs out of the pattern. When a pattern changes significantly then if we have trained ourselves to be "aware" of these patterns, we then become "alert" to the change. Thus individuals can become alert either to the fact that there are patterns or to the fact that the patterns are different.

This ability to be alert is most important when there is a need to be guarded, vigilant or cautious due to circumstances. How does it relate to trust? If someone is trusted because of a known characteristic such as honesty, and suddenly engages in a significant dishonest act of any kind, then it would be crucial to be alert to the dishonest act. In order to address this situation effectively, the dishonest act needs to be confronted in a timely manner. The motivation for the dishonest act needs to be addressed in order to prevent some serious consequences. As we discussed, honesty is the most valuable of all the descriptors where trust is concerned, because without honesty you can't have trust. Addressing the situation soon can also open the door for honest and constructive conversation and actions that can lead to a more positive result than what would have occurred if the situation hadn't been detected or one hadn't been "alerted" to it initially.

Being alert also leads to self-awareness, which in turn leads to self-knowledge. Not only is it important to be alert to situations around us, but also to situations that may exist within us. When we are alert to our own internal patterns, we are much more apt to be attentive to patterns or disruptions to patterns around us, both in other people and in situations. The second "A" of this approach is significant in the process of establishing or maintaining trust.

Third "A" – Action

Only after we have gained the self-confidence that comes from educating ourselves about people and situations (awareness) and noticing patterns and differences around us (alertness) should we take any action. Action taken without being aware and alert to people and situations will more than likely be faulty and/or doomed to failure. Any action we take in a situation needs to have been well thought out. Engaging in education (awareness) and observing the world around us (alertness) does not guarantee success in any action we take, but it definitely minimizes the possibility of failure.

Before taking any action, it's so important to think it through. If I do this, what will be the most likely result? What are the consequences of this action? How will this action improve my life? How will it affect those around me? These are important questions that need to be asked before taking action. Thinking things through is crucial to effective decision-making in any action plan. Another aspect of taking action is the "how" of taking action. Two people can take the same action in similar circumstances; one is successful and the other fails. The difference in the results depends on whether the situation was well analyzed and the approach selected best suited to the circumstances. Approaching a situation by analyzing it and understanding what would achieve the most positive results is obviously better than reacting without thinking things through. Astuteness is the best quality to hone when taking action in any kind of situation. How someone chooses to approach the action and deliver the action can determine success or failure.

CRITICAL THINKING SKILLS

This is the most important skill required when making decisions about trust. If you've ever wondered while watching a TV show or reading a human interest story in the newspaper, why people have engaged in some action that defies common sense, it is most likely because the people involved did not think things through…they did not employ effective critical thinking skills. Critical thinking skills are important in every area of our lives, yet it's the one area that most people don't strive to develop and sharpen throughout their lives.

What do we mean by critical thinking skills? A formal definition could be: the mental process of actively and skillfully conceptualizing, applying, analyzing, synthesizing, and evaluating information to reach an answer or conclusion. Simply put, critical thinking is the ability to think clearly and rationally and engage in reflective and (very importantly) independent thinking. If one is thinking critically they will: 1) make logical connections between ideas, 2) accurately evaluate arguments (such as practiced in meaningful debates), 3) identify the relevance and importance of ideas, 4) solve problems in an organized fashion and 5) something we have been stressing in our discussions throughout this book, reflect on the justification of one's own beliefs and values.

The following are attributes of a critical thinker: One who listens well; one who asks pertinent questions; one who assesses statements and arguments; one who is willing to examine beliefs, assumptions, and opinions and weigh them against facts; one who suspends judgment until all the facts have been gathered and considered; and finally one who examines problems closely and is able and willing to reject information that is incorrect and/or irrelevant. So we have to reach a conclusion that critical thinking implies questioning and evaluating issues and facts, as well as keeping oneself informed and knowledgeable of these issues and facts. A critical thinker must also develop the ability to make counter arguments. A form of counter argument would be a debate, well thought out and well monitored of course, that forces the issue of looking at both sides.

Another way to define critical thinking is to note that it refers to the thought processes used to evaluate information, and the practice of using the results of said evaluation to guide behavior. It essentially means "thinking things through" so that your thinking process is logical, probable, rational, valid and reasonable, and the result of your thinking can be depended upon to make a decision. If, for instance, an acquaintance of yours is always late for a meeting you set with them and you continue to set meetings with them thinking that this time they won't be late, then you are not engaging in critical thinking skills. This example violates the 'dependability' trust factor. Another example is a case where a coworker always exaggerates and changes the facts in situations that happened at work, and yet the next time you talk with him/her you're thinking this time the person won't exaggerate or change facts. Again, this is an example of poor critical thinking skills. This example violates the expectation of consistency and ultimately honesty, that only the truth, the whole truth and nothing but the truth will be shared when in fact it is not.

In both these examples the expectations are that something different will occur when the same set of facts are repeated. But how different is it when it's not the same set of facts? Perhaps the acquaintance you're meeting is sometimes late and sometimes prompt…what then? Perhaps the coworker exaggerates sometimes and not others? How do you judge your trust level with that person? Obviously, it's much more difficult to reach a decision when the facts differ from time to time. It requires an honest, in-depth look at what's occurring. It's at times such as these that it's very important to have honed your critical thinking skills. The examples given are not very consequential…the stakes aren't high in either case. Nothing terrible will happen…annoyance maybe, but nothing serious. But what happens when the decision you must make about trust is very important?

As mentioned with our discussion on the Triple A Approach, the need for educating oneself is paramount. But critical thinking skills go beyond just gathering facts. They include an assessment of the facts in a neutral, objective manner. Consequently, critical thinking skills will always involve looking at an issue from all angles. A one-sided look at any issue will never reflect effective critical thinking skills, and one will never arrive at a logical, well thought out conclusion. A well-noted example of this type of thinking can be seen at election time, when voters profess their full support for one candidate without ever objectively considering what the other candidate represents. Also, these voters stand on one side of an issue without ever considering the other side of the issue. In order to think effectively, both sides of every issue, both sides of every decision to trust, and both sides of believing in a leader must be considered, weighed and analyzed before arriving at a decision. In the academic arena, students can be considered to have demonstrated effective critical thinking skills in a research paper when they: 1) define their terms, 2) provide appropriate and relevant examples, and 3) engage in an analysis that includes compare and contrast type discussions in which many issues are considered and either accepted or denied. Likewise, if everyone would engage in these skills in the trust arena, there would be more enduring trust relationships existing in our daily lives.

EMOTIONAL INTELLIGENCE

History. A third skill to be developed that can be of great assistance in making solid trust decisions is the use of emotional intelligence. Peter Salovey of Yale and John Mayer of the University of New Hampshire coined the term "emotional intelligence" in 1990. The term was popularized by Daniel Goleman's book entitled "Emotional Intelligence." Salovey and Mayer defined emotional intelligence in terms of being able to monitor and regulate one's own and other's feelings, and to use feelings to guide thought and action. Goleman essentially agrees with the former definition but also includes the capacity for recognizing our own feelings and those of others, for motivating ourselves, and for managing emotions well in ourselves and in our relationships. As it indicates, emotional intelligence is the intelligent use of emotions.

Feelings vs. Emotions. Now it is important that we talk about emotions. Emotions of course involve feelings. Looking back in our past culture where certain feelings such as sorrow and grief were thought of as something to be controlled and not expressed in any way....a sign of weakness. Fortunately, we have progressed to the understanding that feelings which give rise to emotions can be both powerful and valuable if expressed constructively...as opposed to destructively. In this context, it is not our intent to render a scholarly distinction between emotions and feelings but rather to gain the understanding that they are connected. Suffice it to say, that feeling is basically the sensation one experiences in a particular situation or place and emotion is an affective state of consciousness in which feelings – joy, sorry, fear, love, hate, etc. are experienced.

The intelligent use of emotions would imply that we recognize our feelings and are not always surprised by them when they make themselves known, as occasionally our feelings can tend to surprise us. Whether you're mad, sad or glad, it is a natural expression of the circumstance. How you choose to express these emotions and feelings is what makes the difference as to whether these feelings are constructive or destructive. It also translates into the intelligent way to manage your emotions. Recognizing and understanding emotions goes a long way in assisting us to manage our emotions. When it comes to trust, we can't always go with just our feelings. Recognizing our feelings and then engaging in a combination of the Triple A Approach, engaging in critical thinking skills and following an emotional intelligence path could lead us to the most effective decision-making process in trusting others.

Application of Emotional Intelligence, Triple A Approach and Critical Thinking skills leads to successful Trust Decision-Making.

It makes "common sense" to employ the intelligent use of emotions as a way to assist in knowing if and when to trust someone. For instance, consider the feeling of someone who is "in love" with another. The tendency is to automatically trust the other person. However, it is crucial to be aware of and to admit to oneself that it doesn't automatically follow that a person is trustworthy because someone is "in love" with him/her. The Triple A approach would say that there's some homework to be done by the person "in love" in the form of educating and gaining knowledge about the loved one. Being "aware" and "alert" can include applying the trust factors to the "loved one" to gain some knowledge about how honest, committed, sincere, dependable, consistent, loyal and faithful the loved one is. This step takes one closer to making a good choice in the decision to trust. Your critical thinking skills come into play when you are alert and gaining understanding by listening, asking pertinent questions (specifically when the person tends to be secretive), suspending judgment until all the facts have been gathered and being willing to reject information that is incorrect or irrelevant.

SUMMARY

As I have stated, my purpose in writing this book is to inspire readers to look at the role trust plays in their lives. I would encourage all readers to strive towards knowing and being able to state: "This is my understanding of trust, and this is how I define trust in my own life." Having this knowledge is foundational to making good trust decisions that result in successful and healthy relationships.

As has been stated repeatedly, we live in rapidly changing times and those of us who educate ourselves on those issues that are important to our survival will gain the confidence and self-esteem needed to process those changes effectively.

I look forward to reading about your progress through your comments on the www.trustontrial.com website.